AND GREAT SHALL BE YOUR REWARD:

THE ORIGINS OF CHRISTIAN VIEWS OF SALVATION

BY

PAUL S. MINEAR

Wipf & Stock
PUBLISHERS
Eugene, Oregon

Wipf and Stock Publishers
199 W 8th Ave, Suite 3
Eugene, OR 97401

And Great Shall Be Your Reward
The Origins of Christian Views of Salvation
By Minear, Paul S.
Copyright©1941 by Minear, Paul S.
ISBN: 1-59752-193-0
Publication date 5/16/2005
Previously published by Yale University Press, 1941

CONTENTS

PREFACE   v

I. REWARDS IN JUDAISM   1
   A. The Basic Pattern of Expectation   1
   B. The First Extension of the Field of Reward   3
   C. The Failure of Expectation and Initial Rationalizations   4
   D. Failure Intensified and New Solutions   9
   E. Summary   13

II. SALVATION IN HELLENISTIC CULTURE   18
   A. Common Presuppositions   18
   B. The Impact of Cultural Anarchy   19
   C. The Stoic Idea of Reward   20
   D. The Gospel of the Mystery Religions   24
   E. Weaknesses of the Hellenistic Pattern   26

III. JEWISH EFFORTS AT SYNCRETISM   29
   A. Stoic-Jewish Amalgams   29
   B. The Fusion of Judaism with the Mysteries   32
   C. The Success of Syncretism   38

IV. THE GOSPEL OF JESUS   40
   A. The Environment of Jesus   40
   B. The Fundamentals of Jesus' Religion   43
   C. Reward in the Religion of Jesus   44
   D. The Kingdom as Present Reality   50
   E. Objections to this Interpretation   52

V. THE EARLY CHRISTIAN SYNTHESIS   54
   A. The Initial Reinterpretation   54
   B. The Pauline Synthesis   55
      1. Apocalypticism Modified   55
      2. Mystical Regeneration Modified 58
      3. The Process of Fusion   62
   C. Early Failures to Maintain the Synthesis   66
      1. Apocalypticism Unmodified   66
      2. Regeneration Unmodified   67

EPILOGUE   69

PREFACE

MEN are today desperately aware of evils from which deliverance is imperative. The immediate outlook for society is so black that few can remain in dilettante indifference to the fateful consequences of human decision. Whether war comes next month or next year, men realize that national conflict is implicit in the structure of our civilization. Whether or not the contradictions of a decadent capitalism lead to overt class war, none can escape the repercussions of actual economic struggle. The stress and strain of the search for bread, for justice and for peace multiply the tensions to which the moral consciousness is subject. For in a time when decision is necessary men are uncertain of the ground upon which decision rests. The shift in the foundations of existence has been too radical, the decay of traditions too far advanced, the shape of things to come too obscure for man's conscience to rest in peace. Dependent upon conditions beyond his control, the individual's quest for the secure and abundant life is subjected to innumerable hazards and frustrations.

But while men are feverishly seeking deliverance from real and potential evils, never have they been more confused or more baffled in defining the ultimate end toward which they strive. Their ideas of the rewards to be sought and expected are as tangled as the skein of life itself. Every conceivable inducement is being advanced by advertisers, psychologists, politicians, teachers, organizers, and ministers. The world is a mammoth Union Square in which evangelists of every creed and every god shout their wares to believers and scoffers alike. The kaleidoscope of rewards which they offer serves to reflect and intensify the confusion of tongues.

How is the intelligent man to discover a path out of the labyrinth that does not end in a cul-de-sac? What is the true goal of his life? How may it be sought with confidence that it will be found? Upon what does success depend? Are the basic rewards of behavior this-worldly or other-worldly, individual or social, tangible or intangible, subjective or objective, historical or super-historical? How are they related to the immediate needs of men? Such questions are unavoidable, and no simple answers will suffice. To be intelligent, the search for enduring values requires a constant advance on many fronts: the analysis of the total relation of an individual to the whole of his environment; the investigation of the complex interplay of economic, political, and cultural forces in the weaving of destiny; the understanding of the range of choice open to the individual; the examination of probable consequences of alternative lines of action; the testing of validity of competing programs of salvation; and the evaluation of historical social experience in the successes and failures of such programs.

One of these prerequisites is the appreciation of the interrelatedness of current culture; an equally necessary condition is the analysis of the historical origin and growth of that culture. For it is the child of earlier civilizations, inheriting from them many of its distinctive characteristics. The ancestral societies have furnished the patterns in which men today formulate their desires, express their needs, and define their values. This heritage has been handed down through the medium of social institutions which bridge the chasm of the centuries by the use of a common tradition.

More specifically, the gospels of salvation current in the modern western world reveal signs of their ancestry in institutional traditions inherited from the Graeco-Roman civilization. Probably the most influential of these traditions has been preserved through the continuing life of Christianity. The Christian doctrines of reward, today operating both inside and outside the church, have been inherited, in more or less direct fashion, from doctrines current in the church in that earlier period. This is not to say that an isolated doctrine has its own separate history that can be completely disentangled from the life of men who produced and used that doctrine. Nevertheless it is not too much to say that, indigenous to the culture of the Hellenistic world, there evolved distinctive configurations of ideas of reward which fulfilled definite functions in the life of that world and which vitally condition the modern perspectives. If this be true, as a clarification of the modern confusion of tongues, it should be worth while to investigate the origin of Christian views of reward, to analyze their function in early society, and to assess their values and defects as related to the life of that society.

Such a task is not easily accomplished, however, for the ideas of reward then were as confused and intricately meshed within the total life of society as they are now. Then, as now, Christianity was a dynamic historical movement, itself the heir of many preceding traditions, each with a distinctive view of salvation. Consequently, the study of Christian ideas necessitates the study of (1) the history of Jewish thought antecedent to the rise of Christianity, (2) the nature of Hellenistic patterns of expectation, (3) the process of fusion of these two streams of thought by Hellenistic Jews, and (4) the definition and development of Christian concepts in relation to the emergent needs of the early Christian communities.

The author takes for granted the fact that all religion appeals to human motives in terms of inducements to faith and obedience. All religion promises values to adherents, a desired and desirable change in their situation. The appeal to reward is present, though often disguised or submerged. Nevertheless, the author is acutely conscious of the dangers of focusing attention upon this one element apart from the other constituents of religious thought and life. To focus attention upon the promised values may lead to a perversion of high religion in any one of several directions. It may unconsciously lead to the view that religion is nothing more than a quest for individual reward regardless of the character and demands of God, that salvation is purely a matter of self-help, that religion is simply a tool for human attainment, that religion does not at times call upon man to transvalue his own values or even to renounce his own desires completely. Religion may corroborate man's sense of highest social values but it may also summon them to judgment before a transcendent God. Moreover, to separate the end-product of salvation, the reward, from the motive and means of salvation does violence to the truly religious consciousness. We have dealt in this book with the results of the salvation process, but not without misgiving, for the validity of the results depends upon so many factors other than the specific content of this saved life. Two men may seek the same reward, but on such different grounds and through such different means that the two quests are not comparable.

This book is based upon a dissertation presented to the faculty of the Graduate School of Yale University in partial fulfilment of the requirements for the degree of Doctor of Philosophy. The title of that dissertation was "The Development of Ethical Sanctions in Judaism, Hellenism, and Early Christianity." In the preparation of this present study, the dissertation has been condensed, supplemented, and rewritten. The basic conclusions have been presented, but they have been cast into a different framework, and much of the evidence supporting them has been relegated to the footnotes.

The author wishes to express his deep appreciation to Professors J. Y. Campbell and Carl H. Kraeling, under whose guidance the initial study was conducted.

PAUL S. MINEAR

Evanston, Illinois
March 1, 1941

AND GREAT SHALL BE YOUR REWARD

CHAPTER I

Rewards in Judaism

A RECENT and provocative statement of a philosophy of history, *The Clue to History* by John Macmurray, presents a series of striking arguments. Christianity is the motive force behind the development of our civilization, but Christianity itself is the product of the Jewish mind and this origin determines the essential nature of Christianity. For the Jews the actual world of social history is interpreted religiously in terms of the activity of God. Through continuous reflection upon contemporary history in the light of past experience, they come to apprehend the true nature and purpose of God. The intention of God is known: "a universal community of persons, with freedom and equality as its structural principles of relationship." Jesus fulfills the process of Jewish history by defining with finality the meaning and direction of this intention. Human activity that denies this intention is self-defeating. Ultimately the establishment of God's kingdom is inevitable.[1]

However satisfactory this position may be judged to be, it illustrates a fruitful point of approach for the evaluation of Jewish thought. In the first place, it indicates the direct bearing of early Christian views of salvation upon the crucial issues of modern society, for, as Professor Macmurray points out, this conception of the goal of history is not only implicit in Jewish and Christian thought but also operates within such secular philosophies as that of Marxism. In the second place, it accents the importance of the Jewish roots of the Christian philosophy of history and the continuing vitality of those roots. Finally, it serves to focus attention upon the really distinctive elements in the Hebrew religious consciousness, the elements which conditioned all Jewish hopes of historical fulfilment.

A. The Basic Pattern of Expectation.

During the eight centuries before Jesus, Jewish hopes of reward remained in close contact with the changing fortunes of the people. As religion was for them a way of living the whole of life and a way of interpreting the whole of history, each historical event and each succeeding situation influenced their expectation of reward. The constant process of adjusting promises to fit immediate needs undoubtedly contributed to the vitality of Judaism. But through all the mutations occasioned by the course of events the Jews refused to surrender their basic faith. Tolerant toward all the emerging desires of men,

---

1. John Macmurray, *The Clue to History* (New York, 1939), chaps. ii, iii.

Judaism remained intolerant toward any attack upon its central convictions. Absolutely fundamental is faith in the reality and power of God, who as Creator and Redeemer is seen to be actively at work within history to bring to fruition his own purpose. This purpose has been effective within the total range of human life in this world and has been definitively revealed in the covenant which he sealed with his people. They have accepted the obligation of complete obedience to his will and he has promised them deliverance from evil and the fulfilment of their national destiny. Acceptance of divine demand means participation in divine deliverance. Confidence in God's power and integrity, trust in his covenant as revealing his historical purposes—these constitute the basis for expectation of just recompense. And since both God's will and man's life are realized in the social history of this world, and because man's personality includes body and soul inseparably, the rewards for righteousness are anticipated in the form of concrete, tangible, social, historical goods.

In early times the needs of Israelites were simple and practical, as is natural in a relatively undeveloped stage of culture. Man's existence as an individual was bounded by birth and death. Values were stated in terms of the minimum necessities: food, wealth, health, life itself. In preëxilic literature, there are many evidences that life was not segmented but whole, that spiritual satisfactions were not distinguished from physical satisfactions, and that the whole of life was included within the sphere of religious sanctions.

Individuals, however, were subordinate to the clan, and the clan was subordinate to the nation. Highest values rested in national prosperity. The most potent inducement to loyalty to God was the promise of national advancement. Corporate sin could only lead to national ruin.

Conviction of the validity of this principle impelled the prophets to their vigorous protests. Stirred by catastrophes present or imminent, they attacked the sins of their people—idolatry, profligacy, greed, injustice—confident that these sins were provoking God's wrath, and that national calamities could be avoided only by repentance.[2] They begged their people to purify their lives, restore justice and mercy, and renew their allegiance to God. The inducement was clear: "Seek good and not evil, that ye may live; and so Jahveh, the God of Hosts, will be with you."[3]

The prophets differed from the people only in their interpretations of God's demands and his future activity. They agreed that obedience to God paid high dividends, that the results of righteousness were concrete, corporate, and certain.[4]

---

2. Amos 2.2–16; Isaiah 1.4–31; Hosea 4.10; Micah 2.3–4.3; also John M. P. Smith, *Moral Life of the Hebrews* (Chicago, 1925), p. 75 f.

3. Amos 5.14; also Hosea 6.1; Isaiah 1.19.

4. Smith, *op. cit.*, p. 86; William C. Graham, *The Prophets and Israel's Culture* (Chicago, 1934), pp. 56–57.

B. The First Extension of the Field of Reward.

The first major amendment to this pattern of thought was the emergence of individual salvation as partially distinct from national destiny. This change was due in part to the maturing moral consciousness of prophetic leaders as they sensed the extreme differences in righteousness among their fellow Israelites. But the immediate historical stimulus was the Babylonian exile. The removal of the Jewish community to Babylon created new needs and submerged old ones. Geographical separation from the homeland and relative happiness in the new colony weaned many away from nationalism. The desire for national success tended to evaporate, to be replaced by the desire for individual welfare. In the earlier period the righteousness of an individual could neither save him from the doom falling upon the nation nor free him from the sins of his parents. Wicked men could be prosperous and good men poverty-stricken without raising doubts concerning divine justice. But in the experiences of the exile, it became obvious that a man could shape his own destiny independently of the fate of the nation. "The soul that sinneth, it shall die; if a man be just and do that which is lawful and right . . . he shall surely live."[5] Furthermore, the experience of each individual was dissolved into a mass of isolated deeds, each entailing a separate award. As recompense was supposed to follow conduct in direct proportion to merit, the outward fortunes of every man became an index of his piety.

This revision in attitude contributed directly to the development of legalism. Believing that everyone is quickly repaid for every deed, people feared to displease God by even a minute breach of his sacred law. It became inherently desirable to obey every law, small or great, ceremonial or moral. Moreover, divine punishment was expected for unconscious as well as conscious misdeeds. Therefore, it became desirable to have one's hidden sins revealed in order to escape their consequences. The conception of retribution thus indirectly fostered the growth of inwardness.[6] Nor could the sinner be excused because of ignorance of the law. If he wished to avoid sin and its punishment, he must study the law night and day.

This attitude toward reward is prominent in the book of Proverbs, in which wisdom, the fear of the Lord, and knowledge of the Law, are evaluated in terms of individual profit and loss. Adultery is foolish; its results are bitter as wormwood. Intemperance brings pain and poverty. Murderers who lie in wait for other men's blood are in reality lying in wait for their own. Those who dig ditches for others fall into them; thieves steal their own lives. Whether the penalty comes at the hands of the community or in the form of sickness, accident or death, it is always due to the will of God, a proof of his wisdom, power

---

5. Ezekiel 18; also R. H. Charles, *Critical History of the Doctrine of the Future Life* (2d ed., London, 1913), p. 63.
6. A. O. Lovejoy, "Ethical Inwardness in Jewish Thought," *American Journal of Theology*, XI (1907), 243 f.

and justice. The motif recurs again and again: the righteous prosper, the wicked suffer. The rewards offered by the sages of Proverbs may be condensed into a short list: life, health, wealth, honor, peace, a large family, and revenge upon enemies. The penalties for vice run parallel: death, pain, poverty, shame, a dying family tree, hatred, and strife.[7]

Proverbs represents the expectation of reward among the teachers and sages; the Chronicler reflects the attitudes dominant in legal and ecclesiastical circles. The basic viewpoint is the same: the dogma of exact retribution unerringly enforced. Only one distinction is to be noted. While Proverbs supports the dogma by reference to contemporary experience, the Chronicler uses the history of the race. In reëditing the stories of the kings of Israel, he introduces suffering as the result of every sin and sin as the direct cause of all suffering.[8] He tells the story of the wars to document the faith that the Lord fights only for those who fight for Him. This faith comes to clearest expression in the speeches attributed to his heroes. "Thou shalt prosper, if thou observe to do the statutes and ordinances which the Lord charged Moses with concerning Israel."[9]

Thus the sanction pattern of Jewish faith implemented the demand for practical morality, encouraged the study of the Law, and colored the interpretation of history. Its persistence attests its power. It was directly adapted to the major needs of men and moulded in terms of concrete and specific values. Its principle operated through the whole area of behavior. It rested for support upon the power, authority and justice of God. It was verified by the history of the race and, for a time, by current events. Failure to meet the test of daily experience proved to be the greatest weakness.

C. The Failure of Expectation and Initial Rationalizations.

The expectation of individual prosperity as a certain reward of piety finds stubborn contradiction in the suffering of the saints. The principle of retribution can be applied more easily to national than to individual experience. When it is applied to the latter, the welfare of individual Jews as pious and patient as Job becomes an almost insuperable obstacle. Continued adversity placed the people in the same dilemma in which the Devil thought he had placed Job. For service of God they had been promised health and wealth and large families. Losing all these, could they do other than ask, "Do we serve God for naught?" "Is God asleep?" "Where is He?" "Is He impotent or unjust?" "Does his promise still hold?" The contradiction of faith by experience moti-

---

7. Proverbs 1.10–19; 2.1–22; 3.1–12; 3.27–35; 4.1–27; 5.1–23; 6.20–35; 7.1–27; 8.10–21, 32–36; 22.22–29; 23.1–35; 24.11–22; 25.8–10, 21 f.; 31.1–9.

8. II Chronicles 16.7–12; 20.14–17; 26.16–20; 28.9–13; 35.20–24. Cf. the list of examples in H. G. Mitchell, *The Ethics of the Old Testament* (Chicago, 1912), pp. 354–356.

9. I Chronicles 22.13. Other speeches with the same purpose are found in I Chronicles 28.8; 29.12 f.; II Chronicles 15.1–7; 16.7–10; 21.12–15; Ezra 9.10–15; Nehemiah 5.13–14.

vates much of the Jewish literature of the last two centuries B.C. and the creative movements of Jewish life are outgrowths of this problem.

The breaking of the fabric of normal expectation became marked soon after the return from exile, when the drift toward social inequality became accentuated and the more pious classes gravitated toward the bottom of the economic scale. The aristocratic and commercial groups began to accumulate fortunes at the expense of the poorer groups, partly as a result of political opportunism and partly through unscrupulous trading practices. The religious conservatives were handicapped by moral inhibitions and racial exclusiveness; they became poorer as the aristocrats became richer. Too true became the saying, "What peace is there between a hyena and a dog, and what peace between the rich and the poor."[10]

Grudging admission that the problem existed and halting attempts to solve it may be found in Ben Sira, who reflects the views of the more prosperous classes. On the whole, he maintained the traditional sanction in all its strength; the certainty of adequate rewards for individual righteousness permeates every part of his teaching. "My son, sow not upon the furrows of unrighteousness and thou shalt not reap them sevenfold."[11]

There are some noteworthy changes in the range of values envisaged, due partly to the growth of urban culture and partly to the sophisticated tastes of Ben Sira himself. As the struggle for physical survival is not for him a matter of everyday concern, his attention can be given to other needs. Escape from death is sought less eagerly than a happy and tranquil death. Length of life is desirable, but a peaceful and joyous life is equally so. To enjoy a happy marriage is as important as to have many descendants. Prestige is to be coveted; few things are worse than to lose one's face with the congregation. The list of compensations for the fear of the Lord includes: desirable furnishings for the house, freedom from criticism, tranquillity of life, a lasting reputation, the respect of enemies, and a large circle of friends.[12]

Proverbs reflected certain tendencies growing out of the traditional pattern of rewards; these tendencies are accelerated in Ben Sira. Greater prominence is given to the need for close adherence to the Law, thus marking a definite stage in the development of legalism which later culminated in rabbinism. To act in conformity to the Law gradually became a sanction in its own right, but the Law gained this independent value through identity with prudential interests and had not, by Sirach's time, severed the bond which united it to

---

10. Sirach 13.18; C. C. McCown, *Genesis of the Social Gospel* (New York, 1929), pp. 268 f.; also Nehemiah 5.1-5; Zechariah 7.10; Malachi 3.5.

11. Sirach 7.1-3; F. C. Porter, "The Religious Ideas of the Book of Ecclesiasticus," *The Old and New Testament Student*, XIII (1891), 89 f. For the use of this sanction to motivate almsgiving, cf. Sirach 7.3; 31.11; 35.10 f.; 40.17; its use in family morality, cf. 3.3-16; 9.1-9; 26.1-3; 30.1-13; 33.24-31; 42.11; its use as a deterrent from such vices as anger, pride, and strife, cf. 8.1-7; 19.1-3; 20.18-26; 23.7-15; 27.16-21; 31.12-31; 37.27-31.

12. *Idem*, 1.17-30; 4.11-15; 11.15-28; 14.14-16; 15.1-5; 25.3-16; 41.16-24.

those interests.[18] The ideal of wisdom also achieves a position of semi-independence. For the upper class of sophisticated teachers, its possession becomes valuable in its own right, and one of the incentives for obedience to the Law is the desire to gain wisdom. The primary value of wisdom, however, is measured in pragmatic terms. It is an excellent investment, returning dividends in the form of peace, health, wealth, joy, and prestige.[14] The "merit system" of accumulating reserves of rewards or penalties is more highly organized in Ben Sira than in Proverbs.

On the other hand, Ben Sira was more aware of the failures of the sanction system than were the authors of Proverbs, and he makes halting and half-hearted attempts to square theory with experience. The challenge of scoffers who denied the efficacy of righteousness led him to advance two different arguments. In the first place, he contended that suffering saints would be compensated by the survival of their name and the number of their descendants. He was not the first to emphasize the persistence of a man's personality in his children, for the early codes of law had taught that a reward to children was a reward to their fathers. But in these earlier writings the idea is a corollary of the belief that the clan was the true unit of society; the promise of rewarding descendants is attractive because of the high value placed upon the survival of the clan. Ben Sira, on the other hand, is an individualist, who emphasizes the reward to the children as an escape from the dilemma created by the suffering of the fathers.

The use of this incentive to righteousness is supported by an appeal to history. In his eulogy of ancient worthies he stresses the immortality provided by their good name and the successful line of descendants.

> Their seed shall remain forever,
> And their glory shall not be blotted out,
> And their name shall live to all generations.[15]

But what about the saint who dies prematurely without descendants? Here the resourceful Ben Sira falls back upon a second line of defence. For those whose life has been full of undeserved suffering, the day of death becomes the scene of the long-postponed judgment. In a single hour of delight a lifetime of suffering fades into oblivion; conversely, in a few moments of terrible remorse, the sinner compensates for all his unmerited happiness.[16]

This recognition of the frequent postponement of justice contributes to the rise of another incentive to piety, i.e., the promise of atonement for former

---

13. *Idem*, 29.9; 19.13 f.; C. G. Montefiore, *Rabbinic Literature and Gospel Teachings* (London, 1930), pp. 279–320; S. Schechter, *Some Aspects of Rabbinic Theology* (New York, 1909), pp. 261–275; G. F. Moore, *Judaism* (Cambridge, 1927), II, 89 ff.; A. Marmorstein, *Doctrine of Merits in Old Rabbinical Literature* (London, 1920), p. 2 ff.

14. Sirach, 1.16–20; 11.1; 15.5–6; 20.27; 24.19, 33; 25.6–11; 39.9–10; 51.21–30.

15. *Idem*, 44.7–15; 41.6–15; 39.11.

16. *Idem*, 11.15–28. F. C. Porter, *op. cit.*, XIII (1891), 90 f.

sins. As unpunished sins increase the store of troubles laid up for the future, men need to cancel these accumulated penalties by an excess of good deeds. As sun melts the ice so good deeds melt the store of postponed punishments. Thus the doctrine of merits created the problem of postponed rewards; and the fear of future penalties necessitated the doctrine of atonement; and the doctrine of atonement, in turn, accentuated the doctrine of merits.[17]

Thus, while this orthodox teacher grudgingly admitted the fact of undeserved suffering, his attempts to defend the traditional pattern of expectation merely rendered the problem more acute. The widening chasm between rich and poor could be rationalized more easily by the well-to-do than by the "ill-to-do." This is illustrated by the poignant struggles of the Psalmists with the same problem.

To be sure, in many Psalms, one finds the dogged reiteration of customary doctrine. These Psalms seem to have been written by those whose lines have fallen in pleasant places, who dwell in ease, confident of a happy life and a large posterity. To them, the promises of reward are fulfilled without error. The pious inherit the land, have abundance to eat, enjoy peace, and die in happiness leaving an eternal inheritance.[18]

Other Psalmists, however, felt the cruelties of harsh economic and social conditions and recoiled against prevalent injustices. Continued suffering caused them to identify poverty and piety, and the prosperity of their oppressors caused them to identify wealth and wickedness, a striking reversal of traditional theories. But while the pious poor of the Psalms were more sensitive to the gravity of the problem, they contributed little more than Ben Sira to its ultimate solution. On the one hand, they believed that the justice denied the fathers would be given their children; on the other, they looked forward to delayed restitution within their own life-time. "Hope thou in God, for I shall yet praise Him." To the extent that they recognize the miscarriage of justice not to an isolated Job, but to the whole class of "patriarchal pietists," to that extent they look forward to justification in terms of a nationwide reversal of fortunes: the pious poor will be exalted and the wicked wealthy will be humbled.[19]

Approaching the history of the race from this angle, they discover many precedents of their own plight. On earlier occasions there had been periods during which the wicked had flourished like the "green bay tree" and the righteous had been treated as chaff. Suddenly, however, while the wicked were enjoying their ill-gotten luxury, God had awakened "as one out of sleep" and had hurled "his adversaries backward," granting to his people their

17. *Idem*, 3.3 f., 14 f., 30; 28.1–8; 34.19; 35.2–7.
18. Psalms 1, 2, 15, 16, 19, 24, 25, 26, 30, 33, 89, 103, 112, 128. J. M. P. Smith, *op. cit.*, p. 241.
19. Psalms 6, 9, 10, 12–14, 17, 22, 35, 37, 42–44, 50, 53, 55, 62, 73, 74, 77, 88, 94. McCown, *op. cit.*, p. 265 f.; A. H. McNeile in Charles Gore, *A New Commentary on Holy Scripture* (New York, 1929), p. 343.

rightful inheritance. With confidence in a similar reversal in the near future, the pietists of the Psalms stand fast in their loyalty to God.[20]

The struggle with scepticism reaches an even greater climax in Job and Ecclesiastes. In each book, the orthodox arguments and the sceptic's challenge are presented side by side. In the former book, Job is the doubter and his friends defend the conservative position; in the latter book, the Preacher is the confirmed cynic, and orthodoxy is represented by editorial interpolations.

Like Ben Sira and the Psalmists, Job's friends stubbornly refuse to surrender the traditional doctrine. They diagnose his maladies as due to hidden or conscious sin and prescribe, as remedy, repentance and renewed piety. While they cautiously concede an apparent miscarriage of justice for the poor, they maintain that there is a sufficient recompense, if not in lands and possessions then in repeated deliverance from starvation, in a long life, and multiplied heirs. For this assurance they find sufficient evidence in history.[21]

Job's solution cannot be as simple as theirs. He cannot escape the obvious testimony of his own experience in which pious men suffer and their oppressors prosper. His stout realism leads him sincerely to doubt the justice of God. The glory of Job lies in the maintenance of personal integrity in spite of extreme misfortune and the resultant doubts.[22] But his religious philosophy reflects that same conviction as his friends', i.e., that piety should bring prosperity if God's justice is to be trusted. The story dramatizes not only the strength of Job but also the inflexibility of the orthodox sanction. Paradoxically, it proves the independence of true faith and also the dependence of true faith upon some historical fulfilment.

In stark contrast to Job, the writer of Ecclesiastes is led to discard outright his faith in divine retribution. His sensitiveness to social injustice serves but to deepen his sense of futility. So terrible are the undeserved sufferings of others that he holds the dead to be better off than the living. All hope of social amelioration is doomed to frustration. Scepticism concerning the fulfilment of justice involves scepticism as to the real historical activity of God. When God gives riches or pleasure to men, he has no regard to merit. Wealth and property, social prestige and social immortality, pleasure, and even wisdom itself—all are vanities and a striving after wind. The superficial rationalizations of those interested only in defending accepted doctrines are readily punctured by this arch-realist. And with the surrender of faith in historical justice is relinquished the essential Jewish faith in God, in national destiny, and in the ultimate fulfilment of the divine covenant.[23]

Conservative teachers were naturally disturbed by this Ingersoll of their

---

20. Psalms 78. Note the difference between this philosophy of history and that of Ben Sira. Note also that Psalms dealing with national rather than individual adversities interpret the same history from the national angle. Cf. Psalms 44.1–23.
21. Job 4.7–8; 5.17–27; 8.8 ff.; 15.13–16.
22. Job 9.13–35; 21.4–34; 27; J. M. P. Smith, *op. cit.*, p. 274.
23. Ecclesiastes 4.1 ff.; 5.19; 6.2.

time who probed so relentlessly into the most vulnerable part of the fabric of their faith. His writing was considered traitorous and was admitted into the canon only after editors had made it palatable by insertions. "Though a sinner do evil a hundred times and prolong his days, yet surely I know that it shall be well with them that fear God."[24]

The whole development thus far indicates the prevalence of a single basic "web of normal expectation" in Jewish faith, its integral relationship to the authority and justice of God, its alleged verification in the history of the race. The primary cause for change was the failure of contemporary experience to fulfil the theory. That Jewish faith successfully denied the implications of this failure indicates that it was based on something stronger than egoistic prudentialism. Only deep personal piety and indestructible faith in the ultimate justice and mercy of God could enable men to remain loyal to God's will in spite of the anguish which seemed to make that loyalty absurd. Nevertheless, the implications of continued failure could not be permanently avoided in the temporizing fashion of Ben Sira, Job and the Psalmists. The pattern of rewards was vulnerable. Ecclesiastes indicates that this weakness was most apparent to those most sensitive to the historical frustration of the hopes of the righteous, and that there was a limit beyond which easy rationalizations would not suffice to keep faith confident and courageous.

D. Failure Intensified and New Solutions.

During the reign of the Seleucids the agonies of pious Jews multiplied. They found themselves sinking still deeper into political, economic, and religious serfdom. A ruthless speed-up was applied to the planned hellenization of Palestine. The ancient propaganda machine undermined the self-assurance of Jewish conservatism. Economic and cultural pressure was employed to lure Jews into apostasy. Finally, under Antiochus Epiphanes, the acceptance of Hellenism was made compulsory and loyalty to the ancestral faith was proscribed. Those most loyal became martyrs. This provided a crisis in faith that could not be met by the easy rationalizations of earlier leaders.

To be sure, the faith of some loyalists was so deeply ingrained that they accepted death rather than its alternative. "All their old ideas of retribution, of compensation to the righteous before death, were shattered by the stern logic of events, and yet they were faithful."[25] Not all of their contemporaries, however, could maintain such heroic faith. The sufferings of the martyrs gave added force to the cynicism of the scoffers and encouraged the spread of apostasy. It was imperative to solve the problem if Judaism were to remain potent.

24. *Idem*, 8.12; 2.26; 3.17.
25. R. H. Kennett, *Composition of the Book of Isaiah* (London, 1910), p. 65; cf. also E. Bevan, ed., *The Legacy of Israel* (Oxford, 1927), pp. 38 f.; J. A. F. Gregg, *Wisdom of Solomon* (Cambridge, 1909), Intro.

Here is the tap-root of apocalyptic thought, the most significant development during the two centuries before Jesus. In all apocalyptic thought the conviction is central that justice will ultimately be reëstablished, though only after the destruction of the present evil age and the divine institution of a new age. Faith in this future historical judgment made possible the most penetrating realism and pessimism concerning the present order without relinquishing confidence in the ultimate triumph of God's historical purposes.

The precise orientation of apocalyptic hope depended upon the immediate form which succeeding crises took. In some periods the chief issue was the unmerited suffering of Israel as a nation at the hand of heathen oppressors. Writers to whom this was the key problem pictured the approaching judgment as a reversal of national fortunes. At other times the problem of the oppression of poor loyalists by rich apostates was uppermost. Writers who grappled with this situation anticipated the reversal of class fortunes. In both of these situations, the problem of individual suffering and martyrdom was usually involved. Consequently most writers pictured a coming judgment in which each individual is assured adequate recompense.

To the writer of the book of Daniel, the sufferings of the nation and the martyrdom of heroic loyalists constituted the issue. Antiochus Epiphanes' program of enforced hellenization threatened the existence of the nation and of righteous Jews who refused to coöperate in his plan. The purpose of Daniel is to inspire loyalty to Judaism by promising glorious rewards for fidelity and terrible penalties for apostasy. Appeal is made to three types of inducement: individual recompense during the present age,[26] individual recompense in the coming age, and national prosperity in the future. The latter two represent departures in Jewish thought.

The keynote of Daniel's visions of the future is the certainty that wicked nations will be destroyed and that Israel will begin her long-awaited kingdom. The only reason for delay in this outcome is the necessity for the period of suffering incurred by Israel's sins to be terminated. This long period of chastisement is almost complete; the golden age is at hand. Under the leadership of "one like unto a son of man," the nation will enter an endless epoch of prosperity. In this mundane utopia, justice will be restored to all; martyrs and traitors who have died before the dawn will be raised to positions of great honor or disgrace. "Many of them that sleep in the dust of the earth shall awake, some to everlasting life, and some to reproaches and everlasting abhorrence."[27]

Much the same prospect is envisaged by other apocalyptists who were struggling with the same emergency. In the Dream-Visions of Enoch, history is rewritten to support prospect with retrospect. The murder of righteous Abel,

---

26. Daniel 1.17; 2.48 f.; 3.8–30; 5.29; 6.3, 22 f.
27. *Idem*, 12.2, 3; 7.12–28; F. C. Porter, *Messages of the Apocalyptical Writers* (New York, 1905), pp. 154 f.

the suffering of good men through the wiles of fallen angels, the oppression of Israel in Egypt—these are examples of miscarriages of justice, but only temporary miscarriages for ultimately the law of recompense comes into operation.[28] The hope of future retribution finds a different support in the Journeys of Enoch. In this book, the patriarch is pictured traveling through earth and heaven where he learns divine secrets and receives direct authorization for his prophecy. His vision of forthcoming judgment centers in the destiny of individuals rather than as in Daniel the revival of the nation. Every soul goes at death to one of four compartments in Sheol. In two of these are placed those who received full retribution during their natural life span; in the other two compartments are lodged the souls of martyrs and apostates to whom justice was not granted before death. Only these latter groups rise for final judgment, martyrs to eternal blessedness, apostates to unending torments.[29]

During the latter part of the second century B.C., the success of the Maccabean rulers in gaining partial independence brought about improved economic and political conditions. The nation was released from heavy tribute; compulsory introduction of Hellenism ceased; a vigorous program of expansion carried Jewish rule into neighboring regions. With the removal of the immediate needs which induced the rise of apocalypticism came the practical neglect of that pattern of thought.[30] It lay dormant during this period of relative prosperity only to spring into new life in the chaotic conditions a few decades later.

Civil strife flamed up in the antagonism of the loyalist Pharisees to the policies of John Hyrcanus in the latter part of his reign (135–104 B.C.). The breach widened during the short rule of Aristobulus because of his political crimes, his advocacy of Hellenism, and his support of the Sadducees. Under Alexander Jannaeus hostility became bitter enmity and civil war broke out with a popular riot in the temple in which six thousand are reported to have been killed. After six years of horrible conflict, the king emerged as victor and proclaimed his triumph by the public execution of some eight hundred opponents.

Supporting Alexander were rich, worldly, priestly aristocrats. Opposing him were strict legalists and pietists, bitter enemies of secular and Hellenistic influences. These loyalists, the natural descendants of the pious poor of the Psalms, suffered constant privation and oppression, in part because of their scrupulous adherence to the traditional faith, all the while wealth and prestige were accruing to their enemies because of their receptivity to Hellenism. It is small wonder that the revival of apocalypticism should be welcomed by these "patriarchal pietists," and that their vision of the future kingdom should center

---

28. I Enoch 83–90.
29. I Enoch 22; cf. also 5.7–9; 10.17; 25.6; 27.
30. Cf. Jubilees and II Maccabees.

in hope for economic and class justice. Writings of the period fluctuate between the prophesying of woes that will befall the luxurious and licentious upper classes and the prophesying of consolations for those who "love God and loved neither gold nor silver nor any of the good things that are in the world." Unjust social divisions in the present age insure a reversal of the fortunes of rich and poor in the coming age. This new pattern of anticipated awards is amply illustrated in the Woes and Consolations of Enoch (I Enoch 91–108), the Parables of Enoch (I Enoch 37–71), and certain sections of the Testaments of the Twelve Patriarchs.[31]

Time marched on, and still the wealthy aristocrats pyramided their position and power; still the humble meek failed to inherit the earth. Suddenly, however, came the calamity of Roman occupation. Immediately the pious poor acclaimed this event as direct punishment of their enemies and as divine revelation of their sins.

> Alien nations ascended thy altar,
> They trampled it proudly with their sandals,
> Because the sons of Jerusalem had defiled the holy things of the Lord.[32]

The Puritans gloried in the fact that the justice of God had been reasserted. They realized, however, that not all wickedness is similarly punished. Impious men who remained prosperous had stored up for themselves "grapes of wrath": hunger, penury, childlessness, troubled sleeping, business failure, and dishonor in the coming age.[33] The exploited righteous, on the other hand,

> . . . shall rise to life eternal;
> And their life shall be in the light of the Lord,
> And shall come to an end no more.[34]

From the time of Pompey on, the fortunes of the nation and of the pietists within the nation continued to decline, providing fertile soil for the growth of apocalyptic enthusiasm. Two factors in the first century A.D. completed the frustration of the Jews: economic and cultural impoverishment attending the tyrannous rule of Herod the Great and his successors; the demolition of the temple and the holy city. Both deepened the pessimism of the pious and helped to solidify their faith in a new age.

In the Secrets of Enoch, the pattern of expectation becomes almost exclusively apocalyptic and individual. Suffering in this era is never punishment for sin, but executes the predetermined lot of man and provides the supreme test of his faithfulness. All vengeance awaits a single great judgment day, in which

---

31. The Testaments of the Twelve Patriarchs are a composite work representing probably a Sadducean original, reëdited by Pharisees, at the period under consideration, and later adapted to Christian usage by interpolations. For evidence of the apocalyptic attitude, cf. T.Jud. 25.4; T.L. 3.1 f.; T.Z. 10.3; T.G. 7.5.
32. Psalms of Solomon 2.2 f.; also 8.1–30; 17.6–10.
33. *Idem*, 2.37–39; 3.14–16; 4.16 f.; 15.9.   34. *Idem*, 3.3–9, 16; 5.9 f.; 6.8 f.; 14.2 f.

"everyone shall learn his own measure and according to his own measure shall take his reward." In the interim, the poor gain merit by being content with their burdens and the rich gain merit by good deeds, unless they complain of their duty or look with contempt on the poor.[35]

A similar quietism, resting upon absolute pessimism concerning the existing order and an absolute optimism concerning the coming order, is found in the Assumption of Moses. This writer interprets history to prove that never has the retribution theory been placed in operation. Justice will be effected only in the kingdom of God, when the righteous men of all ages will be avenged.[36]

E. Summary.

In this complete reversal of the sanction system of early Judaism we come to the end of a long evolution of thought, a process in which each mutation was conditioned by the problem of unfulfilled expectation. In the beginning just recompense was expected promptly following each deed. When experience demonstrated the fallacy of this belief, teachers postponed some awards until later in life, and again postponed them to the day of death and to succeeding generations. When martyrdom destroyed this faith, the promise of selective resurrection was adopted. Once introduced, the scope of this type of retribution was enlarged to include increasing numbers of men and to cover an increasing proportion of their deeds. Finally, the hope of any justice in this age was relinquished, being supplanted by faith in a day of universal judgment. The evolution of national hopes follows analogous stages.

The adoption of an apocalyptic philosophy of history was not a product of philosophical speculation developing according to the laws of logical analysis. Rather, it was the result of age-long human struggle in which old promises failed and new needs emerged. Apocalypticism arose amid the failures of prophetic and legalistic religion, as an effort to provide more adequate support for the ultimate faith by which Israel lived. It is significant that the first definite appeals to post-mortem recompense came at the crisis of martyrdom and were first extended only to those who had not received justice before death. It is also noteworthy that the expectation of a future era developed among those groups which suffered most intensely, and that it was keenest in periods when anguish was deepest.[37] The corporate nature of Judaism is demonstrated by the fact that individual resurrection is uniformly a corollary of social renascence; individual hopes remain dependent upon social hopes. The historical nature of Judaism is likewise demonstrated by the fact that, except in the case of Ecclesiastes, the problem of unfulfilled expectation does

---

35. II Enoch 7.1–5; 10.1–6; 42.1–14; 44.2–5; 50.1–5; 51.1–5; 60.1–5; 66.5–7.
36. Assumption of Moses 10.
37. F. C. Porter, *Messages of the Apocalyptical Writers*, pp. 49 f.; also M. Hughes, *The Ethics of Jewish Apocryphal Literature* (London, n.d.), pp. 75 f.

not lead men to doubt the meaning of history or the reality of the divine purpose operating within history. Human life is social and historical by nature; its true fulfilment can only take place within history, if not now, then in a radical reconstruction of the existing order.

As pessimism concerning the present grew, the "wholly other," transcendental nature of the future age was accentuated. The difference between the two eras was so great that the transition could be made only in terms of divine intervention and catastrophe. When all justice was postponed to this great event, men could interpret present disasters not as divine penalties upon sinners but as the predestined lot of men or as the work of Satan, the king of this age. History is seen as predetermined. Man cannot decide or determine the date of the judgment, or hasten its coming. He can study the earlier periods of history to discover the methods of God's activity, he can examine the ancient prophecies, he can try to discern the signs of the times. But only God can determine the date. Thus faith in future retribution contributed to the millenarian schemes for segmenting history and blueprinting time.

Likewise, the rise of apocalypticism furthered the growth of the doctrine of merits. If recompense is to be delayed, merits and demerits must be recorded until the opening of the books at the final inventory and the accompanying weighing of assets against liabilities. This implied the need for legions of angels as certified accountants to keep the books. It also implied an enlarged importance for the theory of atonement. The Jewish rabbis of the Christian era rejected the social eschatology of the Christians, but retained individual eschatology and the merit system, placing reliance upon the expectation of rewards and punishments after death.

The development of apocalyptic eschatology did not completely supplant the earlier types of expectation. Many Jews continued to reject entirely the thought of resurrection; depending upon retribution in this age (e.g., the Sadducees). Others believed in both present and future recompense; probably only a small minority placed all their reliance upon post-mortem justice. Nor did the sanction of national prosperity disappear with the anticipation of social or personal restitution. In the time of Jesus each of the earlier types of reward survived in the thought of some group. Nevertheless, the apocalyptic ideology represented the most fruitful result of profound grappling with the greatest problem in Jewish experience; it was the product of age-long ethical struggle with the most intransigent facts of human history. Without surrendering the essential insights of prophetic religion, Judaism buttressed them with a mythological interpretation of the future that combined rigorous moral realism and stubborn loyalty to God's historical purpose.

The foregoing treatment of developing Jewish attitudes toward rewards and punishments has necessarily been selective and oversimplified. Some of the causes and results of the mutations have not been discussed. A preponderance of evidence, however, justifies the belief that the steps we have indicated represent the main stream of evolution in this particular area of theology.

This tracing of the main stream indicates the perennial power of the Jewish outlook upon history. Distinctive of Judaism is the living apprehension of the reality of God: a God who is personal, powerful and moral; a God of holiness who places an imperative upon man's conscience; a God of justice whose character is expressed in moral retribution; a God of mercy who redeems man; a God of history whose covenant purposes have been revealed in creation, in past deliverances, in present experience, and in future destiny. Without faith in such a God the Jewish thought of recompense would have been, as Qoheleth said, a "vanity of vanities" and a "striving after wind."

The genius of the Jewish hope likewise rests upon a stubborn affirmation of the unity and solidarity of human personality, an insistence that salvation, to be authentic, must mean a definite change in the status and destiny of the whole man. And such a change must involve the historical realization of salvation for the community, inasmuch as man achieves fulness of life only within the covenant society. Integrally bound up with these primary assumptions are the convictions that man's highest duty is to love God and that expectation of divine help presupposes obedience to divine demands. The promise is based upon the law; only in God's will lies man's peace. The expectation of the kingdom remains true to Jewish faith, for it enshrines the complete confidence in the coming fulfilment of the covenant between God and his elect community, a covenant which preserves ethical demand and divine help in essential interdependence.

Although the survey of developments indicates these elements of power in Jewish hopes, it also raises serious problems which require at least passing consideration.

(1) Is it not apparent that the evolution of hopes is determined purely by economic forces, the idea of salvation being simply the product of the wishful thinking of dissatisfied men, the psychological compensation for cultural frustrations of the poor and the rationalization of the class interests of the rich?

(2) Does not the Jewish doctrine reflect a dominant egoistic prudentialism in which the consequences of every act are coolly calculated from the standpoint of personal advantage to the doer rather than to the recipient? Is religion merely the thinly disguised instrument of the will to power? Does the constant appeal to self-interest reduce the cultus to a "get-rich-quick scheme," in which God and his Law are but the tools of the ambitious?

(3) Is not the stress upon economic prosperity, national honor, and personal advancement as the highest goods an evidence of crass materialism and secularism? Should not high religion deal with things of the spirit, values that are sought for their own sake without concern for consequence?

(4) Does not the experience of men over thirty centuries prove the failure from first to last of this Jewish pattern of expectation, the apocalyptic hope

being the last and most fantastic delusion of all? Does history support the faith in a divine Providence in control of human events, fulfilling promises to men on the level of social destiny? Is not such a unitary philosophy of history incredible, involving as it ultimately does such doctrines as predestination and the periodization of history? Is it not impossible to solve the problem of evil and suffering by simple escape to the future?

These are crucial issues, involving the very foundations of Judaism in its Biblical formulation. It is impossible here to give to them the treatment they merit. But some observations may prevent too hasty and inadequate generalizations. These four objections seem to have more weight at first sight than at second.

(*a*) Economic determinism. The far-reaching influence of economic conditions upon religious ideology has been demonstrated by many authentic studies. Many factors in developing Judaism, however, disprove the theory of complete economic determinism. Let us mention a few. Judaism persistently maintained its independence of contemporary cultures, condemned many of the natural tendencies toward assimilation, produced martyrs and rebellions. Consistently it refused to pander to many desires of men and served to sublimate and to educate those desires. This accomplishment was partly due to the worship of an objective, historical, everlasting God and to the basic fear of the idolatries of men. It was partly due to the fact that this God was holy and righteous, making just moral demands upon men irrespective of their immediate obsessions. Religion was not simply a product of social evolution; it was as well a creative determinant of that evolution. No history of the Jews can ignore this fact. Their faith may have included elements of rationalization and compensation; what phase of human thought does not? But it was also the result of the rapport between men and a larger environment, the crystallization of centuries of human experience of reality.

(*b*) Egoistic prudentialism. Judaism offered salvation, tangible and concrete, but not to individuals as isolated atoms; salvation to persons-in-community. And it demanded that men lose their lives, that they accept loyalty to a reality greater than themselves. The sacrifices of the martyrs indicate that their faith was more than a product of their will to power; their will to power was transcended by a will to obey. It was their faith that God was just and merciful that created the expectation of reward; their desire for egoistic ends did not alone create that faith as a pragmatic tool. It is perhaps inevitable that men should seek to twist reality to suit their own whims, and evidence of that process is clear to any serious student of the problem; but there is equally certain evidence that men sought to bend their wills into conformity with a will not their own. Religion is egoistic, but it is hardly pure prudentialism when its first imperative is to love God with the whole heart.

(*c*) Materialism. That Jews were crass materialists can be maintained only by those who ignore their qualitative cultural achievements. The charge of materialism usually emanates from dualistic schools of thought in which spirit and matter are ruthlessly and unjustifiably separated and made antithetical. To an extreme spiritualist, matter is unreal and any concern for improvement in the standard of living is materialist. The Jew was neither materialist nor spiritualist: he resolutely refused to separate the two. He realized that justice apart from human values and values apart from human needs were unreal abstractions, that a God who takes no interest in the conditions of life or the historical destiny of his children is a God unworthy of trust. The test of high religion is that it should be material without becoming materialistic, secular without becoming secularist. Judaism fulfills these qualifications, as evidenced by the fact that when historical processes failed to fulfill human hopes it did not turn away from history to cosmic speculation, to transcendental spiritualism, or to introvertive mysticism.

(*d*) Historical realism. Even though Judaism may defend itself against these first three charges, can it evade the fourth: have not all of its postponed dreams been frustrate, including its most heroic hope for the kingdom of God in history? The question of the ultimate validity of the Jewish philosophy of history is the most difficult of all. Here, again, it is unrealistic to expect truth without admixture with error. It is also important to remember that Jewish eschatology, like all eschatologies, is forced from the realm of literal description into the realm of mythology in the attempt to describe its conception of the meaning and purpose and end of history. The distinctive values of this philosophy of history can be correctly assessed only in comparison with other philosophies of history current at the time. The ultimate solution of the problem of reward in religion demands an ultimate solution of the problem of history itself. The genius of Judaism in this area can be detected more easily after the discussion of the problem of reward in other cultures and particularly in the Hellenistic. To that field we turn.

CHAPTER II

Salvation in Hellenistic Culture

A. Common Presuppositions.

THE Hellenistic world of the first century was a maze of races, nationalities, cultures, and religions. It included many different streams of development converging and diverging, in striking contrast to the single major stream of tradition within Palestinian Judaism. Many different cults were vying with one another for support, each with its own framework of ideas and its own message of salvation. In Judaism the basic religious doctrines remained constant; in Hellenism, apart from a few philosophical presuppositions, the idea of reward remained fluid. While this variety makes accurate generalizations hazardous, the prevalent attitudes may be suggested, although qualified at many points.

Hellenistic thought may be characterized as anthropocentric. The starting point of philosophical speculation was the question: What is man? What is his true nature? And from early times the answers took dualistic forms. The pattern was set by early Orphics and Pythagoreans who thought of the body as the prison of the soul, which had been originally immortal. Incarceration of the soul in the flesh had resulted from sin. This psychological dualism was a corollary of cosmic and metaphysical dualism. God is the world-soul, the ultimate essence of all being, perfect, unchanging, eternal. The only locale of meaning in the universe is the world of thought, reason, spirit; all else is unreal, corrupt, changing. Hence, the purpose of God is expressed in the nature of the world as it *is* rather than in the achievement of new goals and goods within history. The process of history is indifferent to the realization of true value.

It follows that God does not personally administer rewards and punishments either in this life or in the hereafter.[1] He would be untrue to His nature if He took a controlling part in determining human destiny. Sin is always man's act which entails suffering as a consequence self-chosen and not imposed by divine fiat. Authority for ethical standards and sanctions for ethical conduct are to be found within human experience rather than in divine activity.

As body and soul are separate and as only the soul is immortal and real, so the supreme goods of life refer to the condition of the soul. The welfare of the soul is the home of true value. The normal process of salvation thus follows a different pattern from that of Judaism. In Hellenistic philosophy the highest good is at once its own reward and authority; in Judaism the desired salvation is conferred by God as a reward for human merit. In the former, the process is unified: the motive is desire for the good, the means is the prac-

---

1. G. F. Moore, *History of Religions* (New York, 1919), I, 503; also Plato, *Phaedrus* 109 f.; *Gorgias* 5.23 f.; *Republic* 10.613 f.

tice of the good, the end is the attainment of the good. In the latter, the process is differentiated: the motive is the desire to obey God; the means is a specific program of religious duties; the end is the resulting help which God gives.[2]

But it should not be concluded that, because Hellenistic thought tended to deny to God the giving of rewards and insisted that virtue is its own reward, teachers did not therefore use very attractive inducements for the good life. Their fundamental assumption was belief that the good is always the beneficial and that the highest good is always the greatest happiness.

"If he loves the good, what is it then that he loves?"
"The possession of the good," I said.
"And what does he gain who possesses the good?"
"Happiness," I replied. . . . "Nor is there any need to ask why a man desires happiness. . . . The desire is common to all."[3]

B. The Impact of Cultural Anarchy.

These central assumptions of Greek philosophical schools faced the tests of social experience in much the same way as did the Jewish doctrines of reward. The last three centuries B.C. constituted an age of transition, of sharp social cleavage, of political and religious upheaval. Revolutions—economic, cultural, political, moral, religious—were the order of the day. Civil wars, proscriptions, slave insurrections, imperialistic conquests—all took heavy toll in loss of life, economic debilitation, and the destruction of moral and cultural standards. Included in the debris were the practical disappearance of the middle class, the increase of slavery, wholesale migration of peoples, an acceleration of urbanization, the bankruptcy of the conquered, and the moral disintegration of the conquerors.[4] The wreck of the old social structure occasioned marked tendencies in religious thought.

There was a drift toward accentuated individualism, due to the destruction of the city state and local political institutions. Man's personal needs assumed a larger importance. And with the decay of accepted standards and customs, the individual was forced to look within himself for whatever authority and direction he needed. Religion became highly subjective and introspective.

As local barriers and restrictions fell away the individual found himself in a greatly enlarged world, in which racial and national distinctions were effaced. Communication, travel, the interchange of ideas fostered a cosmopolitan outlook, a tolerance of other religions, and syncretism in the realm of ideas.

Universal suffering engendered a deep pessimism, a pessimism compounded of fatalism and a sense of sin. It was an age of despair: despair of external

2. A. Wolf, "Ethics," *Encyclopedia Britannica* (14th ed.), VIII, 758–761.
3. Plato, *Symposium* 204 f.; *Apology* 29DE, 30A.
4. Virgil, *Georgic* I.505–514; Tacitus, *Histories* 1.2; *Annals* 4.33; Plutarch, *De Defectu Oraculorum* 414A; S. Angus, *Environment of Early Christianity* (New York, 1929), pp. 27–40, 128.

fortunes encouraged a retreat to subjective emotionalism; despair of this world induced a recrudescence of hope in the future world; despair of human powers intensified a dependence upon supernatural intervention.[5] The unpredictability of events stimulated a revival of credulous popular belief in Fate, and in magic, occultism, and astrology as means of influencing one's future. Cut adrift from normal ties, individuals sought within religious associations for consolation and sympathy, fellowship and mutual aid. Moral and social anarchy gave rise to new interest in practical ethics and many moralists appeared with programs of social betterment. In this situation the weaknesses of the older aristocratic and rationalistic philosophies became apparent. Among the earlier philosophies that most successfully met the challenge of these conditions was Stoicism. It typifies the trend away from the aristocratic to the democratic, from the theoretical to the practical, from the metaphysical to the ethical, and from the civic to the individual.

C. The Stoic Idea of Reward.[6]

The Stoics followed the Greek tradition in accepting the desire for happiness as the supreme human motive. The instinct for self-preservation is the earliest and ultimate impulse. "I only pay respect to myself. . . . That is not mere self-love; for it is natural for man to do everything for his own sake; for even the sun does everything for its own sake, and in a word, so does Zeus himself."[7] This instinct seeks the well-being of one's highest and truest nature, i.e., his reason.

The conquest of happiness depends upon a careful discrimination between those objects which are good and those which are bad or indifferent.[8] The wise man never chooses objects that are evil, for they would contradict his nature and prevent his self-realization and happiness. Physical pleasure, social honor, and luxury are deceptive and evil goals of action; the craving for them is a disease. Nor does God use such objects as rewards for righteousness either here or hereafter.

Among the indifferent ends of action the Stoics listed wealth, health, life, friends. None of these was independently good; none should be sought for its

---

5. Plutarch, *De Superstitione;* Lucretius 1.65; 3.991; H. R. Willoughby, *Pagan Regeneration* (Chicago, 1929), pp. 5–9; S. J. Case, *Experience with the Supernatural in Early Christian Times* (New York, 1929), pp. 11–21; S. Dill, *Roman Society from Nero to Marcus Aurelius* (London, 1911), pp. 472–483.

6. For the present purpose attention is centered upon the philosophers of the Middle Stoa: Panaetius, Posidonius, Epictetus, and Seneca. Evidence for their teachings is found not only in the extant writings of the last two named but also in the works of Cicero, Plutarch, and Diogenes Laertius.

7. Epictetus, *Dissertations* 1.19.10 f.; 1.22.1; Cicero, *De Officiis* 3.34; *De Finibus* 3.16; 4.24–26; 5.24; *De Republica* 3.37 f.; Diogenes Laertius 7.85–103; Seneca, *Epistles* 82.15; 87.36; 121.14.

8. Cicero, *De Finibus* 3.36–73.

own sake. Only when they contributed to higher goods were they to be accepted.[9]

The supremely good goal of action, as has been suggested, is the happiness that characterizes the highest development of man's true nature, his reason. "Good men are always happy and bad men are always miserable." The good man is ". . . happy in the highest degree and fortunate and blessed and wealthy and pious and beloved of God and worthy of everything, fit to be a king or general or statesman."[10] The writers of Proverbs had been similarly convinced that the good man is always happy. But happiness to them had been inseparable from external prosperity. To the Stoic, happiness is entirely the product of internal harmony, the complete independence of external fortunes. Happiness can only be secured by seeking the things within one's power, the right mental attitudes.[11] Salvation comes not through a change in the "state of affairs" but in the "state of mind," the creation of a kingdom of heaven within where the individual finds peace and security denied him by external adversity.[12]

The greatest enemies of this coveted peace of mind are the four passions: grief, fear, pleasure, desire. These emotions are irrational impulses, sicknesses of the mind which upset the proper harmony of the soul. Once permitted a place they become "furies infesting the lives of fools." Only by their suppression can peace and tranquillity be assured. Socrates had achieved this happiness and thus had been able to say that although his enemies might kill him, they could never harm him. Such an achievement is possible through complete devotion to that which is within one's own control, one's reason. "This is the magic wand of Hermes. 'Touch what you will,' he says, 'and it will turn to gold.' Nay, bring what you will and I will turn it to good. Bring illness, bring death, bring poverty, bring reviling, bring the utmost peril of the law-court: the wand of Hermes will turn them all to good purpose."[13]

Complete freedom from inner passions and external adversity is the same thing as living in harmony with the law of nature. As the Jews believed that obedience to the Torah insures the greatest reward, so the Stoics believed that obedience to the law of nature would yield the greatest happiness, a parallelism of doctrines recognized by Paul.

> Thus there is one eternal reason in all things,
> Which the wicked of mortals flee from, and yet leave active—
> Ill-fated ones, who long to possess what is useful,

9. *Idem*, 3.43 f.; Seneca, *op. cit.*, 87.31–35; 92.6; Diogenes Laertius 7.102–105.
10. Stobae, *Eclogarum Physicarum et Ethicarum*, II, 200; Diogenes Laertius 7.94–98, 118–122; Cicero, *De Finibus* 3.26–29, 75 f.; 5.71f.; Epictetus, *op. cit.*, 3.10.11; 3.20.15; 4.1.46–50; Seneca, *Epistles* 4.2; 23.1–3; 27.3; 59.1–18; 72.7–12; 85.18.
11. Epictetus, *op. cit.*, 1.1; 3.2; 4.4; Diogenes Laertius 7.9; Seneca, *De Ira* 2.13.2.
12. Epictetus, *op. cit.*, 3.22.26; 3.22.60 f.; 3.24.1–21; *Manual* 19.
13. Epictetus, *Dissertations* 3.20.12; 3.22.60 f.; 3.24.112 f.; 4.1.46–50; Seneca, *De Constantia* 19.1 f.; *De Providentia* 2.6; Diogenes Laertius 7.122; Cicero, *De Finibus* 3.29.

> But will not see, nor hear, that law universal of God,
> To follow which heartily giveth a life that is noble. . . .
> For nothing for men or for gods can be better
> Than ever rightly to honor the law universal.[14]

This universal law is revealed to man in the law of his own being, his reason. Obedience to the law of his own reason is life in accordance with his own highest interest. "To be loyal to the royal" in one's self is to be loyal to God's will. God has committed a spark of divine reason to each man, an orphan which he commands man to care for. "Keep this man for me such as he is born to be, modest, faithful, high-minded, undismayed, free from passion and tumult."[15] In being disloyal to himself, man is disloyal to God. He breaks the law of his own being when he falls into slavery to his passions. "The man who remembers this will be angry with none, indignant with none, revile none, blame none, hate none, offend none."[16]

Universal law is also revealed in the outward course of history for everything that happens happens in accordance with the divine will. Obedience to that will therefore means the calm acceptance of all circumstance. Death comes only at the command of God and man's obligation is simply to prefer whatever comes to pass.[17]

Thus the Stoic answer to the problem of insuring happiness in a chaotic world: retreat to two harbors beyond the reach of storms, the inner kingdom of the spirit over which one can maintain control and the outer realm of universal law whose decrees are eagerly accepted.

The happy life, the life according to reason and natural law, is also synonymous with the virtuous life. "Virtue is a harmonious disposition, choiceworthy for its own sake and not from hope or fear or any external motive. Moreover, it is in virtue that happiness consists; for virtue is the state of mind which tends to make the whole of life harmonious."[18] The virtues are both means and ends for they both cause happiness and help to complete it. It is not inconsistent to seek virtue for the sake of virtue and to seek virtue for the sake of happiness, for virtue and happiness coincide.[19] Here is a paradox similar to that of the Jews who taught that one should serve God through love of Him and at the same time serve God for the sake of reward. In both systems the service of God is at once the most abundant life.

For the Stoic as for the Jew, the service of God implied the service of fel-

---

14. *Hymn of Cleanthes*; Diogenes Laertius 7.87–9.
15. Epictetus, *Dissertations* 2.8; 1.25, 28.
16. *Idem*, 1.28.10; 1.14.14–17; 2.80.20–29; 3.1.25–29; 3.15.8–13; 4.19.17; Diogenes Laertius 7.108 f.; Seneca, *Epistles* 5.4 f.; 8.5; 14.1.
17. Epictetus, *Manual* 53; *Dissertations* 1.12.8–16; 3.13.9–13; 4.1; Seneca, *De Providentia* 5.8 f.
18. Diogenes Laertius 7.89 f.; Cicero, *De Finibus* 3.25 f.; 3.70 f.; *De Officiis* 3.11–29; Seneca, *Epistles* 71.4–6; 117.27; 113.31.
19. Diogenes Laertius 7.89–99; Cicero, *De Officiis* 3.11–29.

lows. As the divine reason indwells the universe the life of reason recognizes the unity and solidarity of mankind. All men share in the divine reason; all have God as a father; all are members of one body and have a common destiny. Everyone is by nature a citizen, a son, a brother; he should act accordingly.[20] "I'm human. So I think no other man a stranger." The life of reason necessitates "humanity, generosity, justice, integrity."

Despite these evidences of high altruism self-interest retained priority over social responsibility.[21] When friends suffer misfortune one must help them, but he must not give way to irrational sentiments of pity or grief. In reality, friends can suffer only from their own attitudes, not from external circumstance. If a citizen hears that robbers are planning an attack on a certain city, he should rush to warn the inhabitants. But if he arrives too late and finds them all killed, he should not give way to pity. All that matters is whether they and others accept that event without sorrow.[22]

The reward to which the Stoic sage appealed, then, is a life of perfect happiness, freedom, self-control, and peace, gained by obedience to the law of nature which is the law of indwelling reason. It is a life of virtue and social responsibility maintained independently of external fortunes. Such a pattern of salvation had elements of strong attraction. To men obsessed with uncertainty and dread it gave confidence and peace. To men grappling with sickness, lonesomeness, poverty, or exile it gave a new independence and contentment. To men seeking release from moral slavery it gave new self-control and power. To men sensitive to social anarchy it gave a thoroughgoing program of reform and a clear-cut code of moral behavior. With all of these it supplied a vital fellowship, a sense of mission, and a constant communion with deity. Authority for this pattern it provided by its analysis of human nature and divine nature. Examples were provided by the stories of great heroes of the past: Socrates, Antisthenes, Diogenes; in fact, the meaning and purpose of history are reduced to that of "biography teaching by example." The evidence of science and history was strengthened by the personal testimony of the Stoic missionaries, in whose enthusiastic and sacrificial lives was contagious power.

These satisfactions, however, were not entirely adequate to meet the religious needs of the masses. Stoicism was a religion of attainment, dependent ultimately upon man's own power and supported by human reason rather than divine revelation. In the emphasis upon reason, it did not give due regard to the emotional or volitional aspects of human nature; in the emphasis upon the individual, it failed to appreciate man's dependence upon the group; in the emphasis upon the goodness of nature and history, it denied the real presence

20. Epictetus, *Dissertations* 2.10, 14, 20; *Manual* 7; Seneca, *De Clementia* 3.4; *De Ira* 2.31; 3.35; Cicero, *De Finibus* 3.62 f.
21. Diogenes Laertius 7.96; Epictetus, *Dissertations* 3.3.6; Seneca, *Epistles* 66.10 f.
22. Seneca, *De Clementia* 2.4–6; Epictetus, *Dissertations* 3.20, 24; 4.1, 6; *Manual* 16; Cicero, *De Finibus* 5.65–70.

of the powers of evil; in the appeal to selected individual heroes in history, it indicated that its goal was possible only to the few. Stoic pantheism was alien to the growing pessimism concerning nature and history; its humanism ran contrary to the growing despair of human power and capacity; its rationalism could not satisfy the urgent demands for emotional assurance nor escape the increasing scepticism of human wisdom; its this-worldliness failed to stem the uprush of other-worldliness. "In its strength was the fatal weakness of Stoicism: it did not deal in supernaturalism, and that was the only coinage that had general acceptance in the first-century world."[23]

D. The Gospel of the Mystery Religions.

The supernaturalism which Stoicism could not consistently accept found expression in the mystery religions. These cults were enjoying a great wave of popularity during the first century, due in part to the correlation between their promises of salvation and the urgent religious demands of the age. All of these cults were cosmopolitan in their appeal and individualistic in their application. All were highly syncretistic and tended to preach much the same gospel.

There was unanimous agreement in the pledge of personal immortality as the highest boon to men. Initiates were granted a "rebirth for eternity."[24] The Eleusinian devotee sings: "Death is for us mortals no longer a bane but a blessing."[25] The follower of Isiac ritual was assured: "As truly as Osiris lives shall he live; as truly as Osiris is not dead shall he not die; as truly as Osiris is not annihilated shall he not be annihilated."[26] The assurance of tortures in the underworld for the uninitiated formed a part of the typical conversion appeal.

The nature of immortality varied. Some cults accented freedom thus gained from the flesh and its passions, some stressed the escape from death and postmortem horrors, some identified immortality with release from the neverending chain of rebirths, some found chief value in the anticipation of unhindered life of mind and spirit. But in all the mysteries, the gift of immortality is reserved only to the blessed as the highest reward for their piety.

The process of regeneration fused many elements of great attractiveness. Since Hellenists thought of time as relatively unreal the gift of immortality was not simply a future event; it could be experienced in the present as well.

---

23. H. R. Willoughby, *op. cit.*, p. 286.
24. Taurobolium formula, *Corpus Inscriptionum Latinarum* vi, 504, 512.
25. *Ephemeris Archaiologike* (1883), p. 82.
26. Erwin Rohde, *Psyche* (New York, 1925), pp. 542–544, 574–578; cf. also Cicero, *De Legibus* 2.14, 36; Plutarch, *De Superstitione* 7; *Hermetica* (Scott) 10.8.19 f.; Plato, *Phaedo* 13, 29, 69c; *Gorgias* 47, 493B; *Republic* 2.6; Orphic burial tablets in J. E. Harrison, *Prolegomena to the Study of Greek Religion* (Cambridge, 1903), pp. 566 f., 670 f.; A. Dieterich, *Eine Mithrasliturgie* (2d ed., Leipzig, 1910), p. 2.

The experience of rebirth was an immediate goal, which met the craving for emotional release. Exhilarating ecstasy accompanied the performance of the rites. The early Dionysiac worship—communion with the god of the vine—led to immortality and intoxication.[27] The performance of the Eleusinian drama lifted men to great heights of excitement. Plutarch compared the joy of initiates to that of exiles returning home.[28]

For many cults, conversion involved participation in the epic drama of a dying-rising savior, who had come to earth as man, who had toiled and suffered with men, who had experienced all the sorrows of human existence culminating in the pains of death, and who had conquered all the demonic powers, thus receiving power to save others. The initiate inherited that power when he participated in the drama of dying and rising.

Regeneration and the consequent immortality were both dependent upon the mediation of divine potencies and immediate union of human and divine elements. Man could only become immortal by entering into deity, by becoming deified. In some cults this process of deification involved the crude practice of eating or drinking the divine substance in a sacramental meal.[29] In others a sacred marriage was celebrated or the initiate was adopted as a child of the deity.[30] Each of the Orphic converts became a Bacchos.[31] In Hermeticism the experience of communion achieves highly spiritualized form, independent of ritual. The union of human *Nous* with divine *Nous* results from the exercise of right knowledge; the planned suppression of the passions opens the way for the reunion of man's light and life with the divine life and light.[32]

The experience of rebirth thus included deliverance from the tyranny of sin and the flesh, a deliverance realized partially in the present and fully "when that which is perfect is come." To the Hellenist sin was implicit in the carnal passions; sin and mortality are corollaries. Immortality is meaningless apart from the conquest of these. The joy of the initiate rested in the fact that he had become "clean from man's vile birth and coffined clay."[33]

Another attraction offered by the mysteries was escape from the power of hostile spiritual forces, astral deities, and the grip of Fate. Men felt themselves helpless in the hands of unseen and hostile "principalities." The only hope lay

---

27. Cf. J. E. Harrison, *op. cit.*, chap. viii; E. Rohde, *op. cit.*, pp. 258 f., 284 f.

28. Plutarch, *De profectu in virtute* 10; *De facie in Orbe Lunae* 28; *Corpus Inscriptionum Latinarum* vi, 142; A. Dieterich, *op. cit.*; E. Rohde, *op. cit.*, pp. 255–260; H. R. Willoughby, *op. cit.*, pp. 266 f.; F. V. Cumont, *Oriental Religions in Roman Paganism* (Chicago, 1911), pp. 44 f.

29. Justin, *Apology* 1.66; Firmicus Maternus, *De errore prof. rel.* 16 ff.; Clement Alex. II, 15; Euripides, *Fragment* 472N; I Corinthians 10.

30. Firmicus Maternus, *De errore prof. rel.* 10, 28, 104; Pausanias 2.11.3; Hippolytus, *Philosophumena* V.8.164–172; A. Dieterich, *op. cit.*, pp. 136 f.; E. Rohde, *op. cit.*, pp. 601–603.

31. Burial tablet, in J. E. Harrison, *op. cit.*, p. 670.

32. *Hermetica* 1.18–20.

33. Euripides, *Fragment* 475; A. Dieterich, *op. cit.*, p. 4, line 5; E. Rohde, *op. cit.*, p. 546; Paul Wendland, "Hellenistic Ideas of Salvation," *American Journal of Theology*, XVII (1913), 346 f.

in gaining the help of a superior lord, who had proved his ability to subdue all other powers. With his help one could throw off the baleful hand of Chance and feel assured of stability, prosperity, and peace.[34]

These, then, are the chief rewards proclaimed by the mysteries; all of them closely allied to the experience of rebirth: an immortal life freed from the necessities of sin, flesh, death, and hostile deities; an immediate experience of union with the divine, authenticated by ecstasy, visions, dramatized revelation, and *gnosis;* a new power of moral control, a new social fellowship and new ability to face the threatening future with inner certainty.[35]

This summary of rewards sought by the mysteries does less than justice to divergences among the cults. In some the stress is upon a refined type of ethical and speculative mysticism, in which contemplation, purification, spiritual communion and elevated *gnosis* are central. In others the stress is upon a cruder type of ritualistic sacrament and orgiastic ecstasy. In still others predominant attention is given to the more practical needs of men: health, wealth, deliverance from calamity, and assurance of economic security. The desire for political stability and material success, however, was usually channeled into the observance of the imperial cult, the decadent state rituals, and the local worship of the traditional deities.

E. Weaknesses of the Hellenistic Pattern.

The gospel of the mysteries possessed many elements of power: it appealed to dominant needs, claimed supernatural authority on the basis of ancient traditions, sought intellectual support by free reference to current scientific concepts, and conveyed emotional certainty through immediate emotional experiences of release, exhilaration, and catharsis. Nevertheless, in spite of these tangible values, all forms of dualistic religion in which Hellenistic culture found expression were permeated by the same glaring defects. Four of these may be suggested, all of which are closely interwoven.

(1) Individualism.

Hellenistic mysteries, following the perspectives of philosophy, dissolved the solidarity of individual and society, thus ignoring the necessary communal basis for the fulfilment of life. The individual becomes the focus of value, the unit of religious relationships, the sole object of salvation. In fact, salvation is possible only to the individual, without respect to social destinies. The demands of brotherhood remain secondary to the demands of selfhood even among the Stoics.

---

34. Cf. A. Dieterich, *op. cit.,* p. 4, line 5 f.; Apuleius, *Metamorphoses* XI.5; B. S. Easton, "Pauline Theology and Hellenism," *American Journal of Theology,* XXI (1917), 367 f.

35. For similar summaries, cf. A. D. Nock, *Conversion* (London, 1933), chap. vii; H. R. Willoughby, *op. cit.,* pp. 265 f.; S. Angus, *Mystery Religions and Christianity* (London, 1925), chap. v.

(2) Subjectivism.

As the locus of reward moves from society to the individual, so the content of the reward moves from the realm of history to the realm of psychology. The solidarity of soul and body is dissolved; values are defined not in terms of external fortunes but in terms of subjective experiences. To affirm the reality of such values requires a concentration upon one's feelings and demands a dualistic view of the universe to prove that the subjective values thus apprehended are integral to the true universe of value. And satisfaction with subjective emotional experience may delude men into believing they have found the fulfilment of life, when in fact such fulfilment has been denied. The flight from life may be rationalized into a false triumph. If the worth of corporate historical goals is denied, religion may become introspective mysticism, world-denying asceticism, enervating quietism, or emotionalistic spiritism. The removal of the check of communal experience opens the way either to ultimate scepticism concerning the values promised by religion or to complete self-deception.

(3) The Separation of God from the World.

We have seen that Stoicism defined happiness in terms of harmony with the natural, universal law of reason. Such happiness, in their view, could be won only by affirming the essential goodness of the physical universe and by accepting every historical event as the decree of Zeus. The world itself needs no redemption; history needs no future culmination to bring its meaning to full fruition. If the world seems evil, what is needed to gain happiness is an effort of thought rather than an effort to change events.

The mysteries, on the other hand, define happiness in terms of escape from a wholly evil world, one that inevitably "goes to the devil." God is wholly removed from contamination by anything physical; the realm of redemption and the realm of historical social existence are disparate and disjunctive. Fatalism concerning the course of events is made inevitable: either they are bound to be good, as in Stoicism, or they are bound to be evil, as in the mysteries. In the latter case salvation necessitates a flight from historical reality; time becomes an illusion. "Nothing really happens in what happens." Only in mystical union with God does one receive salvation, and such a union is by nature timeless. Again the choice seems to lie between scepticism concerning the reward offered or self-deception in being satisfied with the worth of the reward offered.

(4) The Ignoring of Ethical Prerequisites of Reward.

It has been frequently observed that the promise of salvation by the mysteries was not organically related to specific moral demands upon the initiates, that the fulfilment of life was offered without the necessity of fundamental ethical reorientation and behavior of the believer. To be sure, some cults required moral purification and ascetic practices but salvation did not imply the redemption of the whole of life. Likewise, it has been frequently suggested that the reason for this hiatus between conduct and reward is to be found in the sharp dualisms of matter vs. spirit, the world vs. God, time vs. eternity, the individual vs. society. Less frequent has been the observation that the emergence of these dualisms in Greek philosophy was due, in part at least, to the rationalization of economic and political interests by the aristocrats of Greek society who feared and opposed social change in the direction of justice for other groups in their society. Whether or not in their origins the mysteries represented an evasion of ethical and social demands, it is clear that in our period they did not serve as a creative agent for producing social changes that would alleviate human suffering. They were at peace with the political and economic rulers of the day; the men who received power and wealth from their injustices feared no challenge from the cultic leaders. And the absence of conflict indicates again the utter indifference to moral, social, and historical bases for the fulfilment of the good life. A religion that offers refuge from growing perplexities without seeking to remove the causes of those perplexities, that offers deliverance from sin without coming to grips with the chief sources and manifestations of sin, that offers an outlet for individuality without coming into conflict with economic and political forces which deny opportunity for the rich development of personality—such a religion is vulnerable for it offers a salvation that is self-defeating.

A comparison of the Jewish pattern of rewards with the Hellenistic pattern reveals that, while each has defects, they do not share the same defects. Each has distinctive values precisely at the points where the other is weak. In the Jewish development is found the extreme expression of faith in salvation within the historic process in terms of personal-social standards of living. The Greek development reveals the extreme expression of faith in a salvation wholly independent of history and society in terms of inner spiritual values. Is there any *via media*, any synthesis that will enable the retention of the truths of both systems and the elimination of the weaknesses? If there is such a synthesis, surely we may expect to find some historical expression of it. And where should we look for this synthesis if not in the religion of those individuals whose personal heritage includes both?

The investigation of the problem of rewards thus leads to a study of the thought of Dispersion Judaism and of Hellenistic Christianity. Do they present a syncretism in which Greek and Jewish ideas of rewards are added together without the removal of fundamental inconsistencies, or do they indicate a creative process of amalgamation in which a new and more fruitful solution to the problem of salvation may be found?

CHAPTER III

Jewish Efforts at Syncretism

DURING the three centuries before Christ there was constant interaction between Judaism and its Hellenistic environment. From the standpoint of the individual Gentile, Judaism was another Oriental cult competing with other religions of the day for his support. It offered a very definite promise of salvation based upon supernatural guaranties and attainable through obedience to the Law. Hellenistic Jewish leaders found it necessary to appeal to four groups: Jews who had taken up residence outside Palestine, Gentile proselytes, "god-fearers" who attended synagogue services, and wider pagan groups who had not yet been reached. The religious needs of all four groups were affected by the perspectives of Hellenistic culture. The infiltration of Gentile ideas could not be prevented, and the process of infiltration can be observed in the literature produced by these Hellenistic Jewish leaders.

A. Stoic-Jewish Amalgams.

The attempt to combine Stoic and Jewish perspectives is clearly revealed in the Letter of Aristeas. The author seeks to prove to Greek readers the superiority of the Jewish Law in providing the fulfilment of their needs. He defends the supremacy of the Law as the highest manifestation of reason and goodness and as the essential instrument for gaining happiness.[1] He explicitly accepts the basic Stoic principles. All men desire the highest good. Knowledge is the chief means to this end and ignorance the chief cause of failure.[2] Life is a contest between irrational impulses and the reason, a struggle in which every man can attain the exalted rank of kingship by mastering his own passions.[3] Desire for wealth and fame prevents one from being happy. Uncontrolled passions lead to the life of vice where one is dominated by fear, grief, envy, pride, anger, injustice, intemperance and error. These maladies of the soul are the supreme punishments of sin. The fruit of righteousness, on the other hand, is serenity, self-control, inner freedom, the enjoyment of a good conscience, and calm acceptance of whatever fate has in store. Every incentive used by Stoic teachers is found in the Letter, although some find greater emphasis than others. Here we observe Jewish faith moving from its God-centeredness to a new center in man, from an authoritarian basis for ethics to a rationalistic basis. The author insists that Judaism is superior to the philosophers because its starting-point is God, and God alone can fulfill human needs. His awareness of

1. Aristeas 189, 207, 260–261.
2. *Idem*, 127, 189, 195, 210, 252.
3. *Idem*, 130–131, 225, 232, 243–245, 252, 253, 262, 275–278.

that distinction, however, implies that he has already started from Greek presuppositions rather than Jewish.[4]

That the process of assimilation is relatively undeveloped is evidenced by the fact that the traditional Jewish rewards appear alongside the Stoic. Aristeas appeals to the desire for wealth at the same time that he denounces such desire.[5] He maintains that the king's prosperity is a reward for his piety, but assures his readers that God sends good and evil to men regardless of piety.[6] He paints a glowing picture of the king's feasting, but warns against the vices of luxury and pleasure.[7] The careless way in which these contradictory sanctions are superimposed on one another is a sign of syncretism rather than synthesis. The author is obviously a propagandist who is more concerned to make proselytes than to reconcile inner contradictions or to struggle to satisfy his own personal religious needs. Without much awareness of the radical step that he is taking, he assumes that the highest rewards of righteousness are freedom, peace, a good conscience, self-mastery, the fulfilment of virtue, individual happiness.

A similar example of uncritical adjustment is provided by parts of the Testaments of the Twelve Patriarchs.[8] In these sections Stoic doctrines of reward prevail. Man is the battleground between the spirits of Beliar and the spirit of God, between vices and virtues, between the passions and reason. The chief passions are lust, covetousness, jealousy, envy, anger, greed, pride and dishonesty. They carry their own penalty in terms of ignorance, inner confusion, and spiritual death.[9] The patriarchs are presented as types of various sins and the resulting consequences. Reuben testifies to the destructiveness of fornication,[10] Judah describes the penalties of evil desire[11] and Simeon tells of the anguish which envy entailed.[12] The distance between these conceptions and the orthodox Jewish doctrine can be measured by comparing the results of Judah's sin in the Testaments with the earlier account in Jubilees, Chapter 41, and the results of Reuben's sin in the Testaments with the account in Jubilees, Chapter 33.

The supreme reward of virtue is freedom from slavery to the lower, irrational nature of man. The peace which such freedom brings is synonymous with the indwelling presence of God. The picture of the ideal wise man in the Testaments is thoroughly Stoic in both form and content. The sage is completely free from passions, confusion and the desire for corruptible things, such as wealth and pleasure. He is blessed with spotless character, peace of soul, constant rejoicing, and the indwelling presence of the divine. Like the Stoic,

---

4. *Idem*, 200, 235.
5. *Idem*, 205, 255–257.
6. *Idem*, 190, 197, 199.
7. *Idem*, 212, 257, 263.
8. The sections in which Stoic sanctions are most prominent are the following: T.R. 2–4; T.S. 3.1–5.3; T.L. 13; T.Jud. 13–20; T.I. 4.1–7.8; T.Z. 8.4–9.2; T.D. 1.1–5.3; T.N. 1–3; T.G. 3.1–6.4; T.A. 1.3–6.6; T.Jos. 1–10; T.B. 3.1–9.2.
9. T.R. 2.1 f.; 3.3–6; T.Jud. 13.3; 16.1; T.S. 3.1; 4.7; T.D. 2.4; 4.7; 5.1; T.N. 8.4.
10. T.R. 4.6–11; 6.3 f. 11. T.Jud. 13.8; 18.2–6; 14.1–16.5.
12. T.S. 3.6; 4.7 f.

he is free from injury from external misfortune, because he gladly accepts whatever God wills.

> The single-minded man coveteth not gold,
> He overreacheth not his neighbor,
> He longeth not after manifold dainties
> He delighteth not in varied apparel,
> He does not desire to live a long life,
> But waiteth for the will of God [i.e., destiny],
> And the spirits of deceit have no power over him. . . .
> There is no envy in his thoughts, . . .
> And no worry with insatiable desire in his mind.[13]

Few passages in any literature so directly contradict the orthodox Jewish viewpoint as this and few express so accurately the Stoic ideal of the rewards of virtue.

The authority of the divine will is revealed not only in the Torah but also in the order of the universe and in the events which befall men.[14] Man must accept both without the desire for change. This universal law is reflected in the demands for kinship and in the reality of universal brotherhood. All these are reminiscent of current Hellenistic standards.

The author's use and interpretation of history are an index of his Hellenistic spirit. He does not look upon history as the field for divine activity in seeking definite social goals. History simply provides examples to illustrate the Stoic doctrines. Joseph typifies the virtue of moderation and Gad the vice of hatred.[15] Their rewards are wholly independent of social and historical values, wholly conceived in subjective, rationalistic, individualistic terms. This complete reversal of standards of value indicates in these sections a more complete assimilation of Hellenistic patterns of salvation than is found in Aristeas. But it is clear that this assimilation involves the real surrender of Jewish perspectives; here we have no true synthesis, but Stoic preaching from the pen of a Hellenistic Jew.

The process of infiltration at an even more developed stage is apparent in Fourth Maccabees, whose author sets out frankly to vindicate Judaism on the grounds of Hellenistic philosophy. He presents obedience to the Jewish Law as the best means of attaining the rewards sought by the Stoic philosophers—notably self-mastery, the rational virtuous life, freedom from misfortune, pain, and the evil passions.

> For in the day when God created man, he implanted in him his passions and inclinations, and also, at the same time, set the mind on a throne amidst the senses to be his sacred guide in all things; and to the mind he gave the Law, by which if a man

---

13. T.I. 4.2–5; T.B. 6.1–6.   14. T.N. 3.2–5.
15. N. Bentwich, *Hellenism* (Philadelphia, 1919), p. 234; S. Angus, *Religious Quests of the Graeco-Roman World* (London, 1929), p. 56.

order himself, he shall reign over a kingdom that is temperate and just and virtuous and brave.[16]

These are the four virtues of the Stoic teaching which they in turn had received from Plato. Reason is the master-gardener, weeding, pruning, watering and cultivating the dispositions. Reason is guide of the virtues, the bridle of the passions, the helmsman of the ship—all expressed in typically Greek metaphors.[17]

As the Testaments discover the ideal Stoic wise man among the patriarchs, this author finds him in the Maccabean martyrs. When the seven sons were brought before the tyrant and given the choice of torture and death or honor and wealth, each chose to die for the sake of virtue. By their contempt of pain, they proved that reason is superior to the passions, that their will was utterly outside the reach of external compulsions. Throughout their period of torture they were supported by the joys of virtue; their tormentors were suffering far worse anguish than the victims. Of all reasoning minds, they were "more kingly than kings, than freemen more free," "athletes of God" who could not be beaten.[18]

These Hellenistic incentives to piety are not, to be sure, the only sanctions used. A vestige of the old prosperity-piety quotient can be detected, and the appeal to social prestige as reward is apparent.[19] More important, the assurance of immortality for the martyrs implies a similar expectation for all who, like them, suffer for righteousness' sake.[20] Yet these earlier Jewish sanctions are peripheral rather than central. They are due to the earlier account of the martyrdom in Second Maccabees and do not reflect the outlook of the editor of Fourth Maccabees. To him the Stoic sanctions are sufficient support for the practice of Jewish law-observance. In fact, except for his formal allegiance to the Torah, the religion of the author is hardly recognizable as Jewish. He has forsaken distinctively Jewish theology, eschatology, psychology and soteriology in his eagerness to present Judaism as the fulfilment of philosophical ideas and hopes. The result is extreme adaptation of Judaism to Stoicism, not the blending of the two into a new synthesis. The failure of these Jewish writers to effect a synthesis raises doubt about the possibility of such a synthesis.

B. The Fusion of Judaism with the Mysteries.

The ease with which Stoic and Jewish patterns of thought can be distinguished in the above writings indicates that the process of assimilation was both artificial and superficial. In contrast, the difficulty of disentangling the strands

---

16. IV Macc. 2.21–23; cf. Diog. Laertius 7.52 and Wisdom 8.7.
17. IV Macc. 7.1 ff.; 1.6; 3.1–5; cf. R. H. Charles, *Apocrypha and Pseudepigrapha* (Oxford, 1913), II, 662–666 for an extensive list of parallels.
18. IV Macc. 1.8–10; 8.12–29; 10.4–14; 11.21; 13.6; 15.29–16.1; 17.10–12.
19. *Idem*, 3.30; 4.20; 17.14–24; 18.3.
20. *Idem*, 7.18; 12.10–20; 9.1–9; 11.2 f.; 13.14 f.; 18.15–19.

Jewish Efforts at Syncretism

of thought in Jewish writings influenced by the mysteries indicates that here the process of fusion more nearly approached a true synthesis. This in turn suggests that Jewish faith was more compatible with Oriental religions than with Greek philosophies. The process of fusion of Hellenistic Judaism with the Oriental gospels of redemption was facilitated by their common ancestry in primitive Egyptian, Babylonian, and Persian cultures. S. H. Hooke and others have excavated this common substratum of myth and ritual underlying the religions of the Near East.[21] The stage of assimilation which we find in such books as the Wisdom of Solomon and in the writings of Philo presuppose a long tradition of Hellenization, in which Diaspora Jews had become more and more receptive to the goal of religion as envisaged by the mysteries.

The earlier stages have been most completely analyzed by E. R. Goodenough,[22] who discovers traces of the mystery gospel of salvation in the pseudo-Philonic *De Sampsone* and *Biblical Antiquities*, Aristobulus, Alexander Polyhistor, *The Sibylline Oracles*, Artapanus, the pseudo-Justinian *Oratio ad Graecos*, and Jewish liturgical fragments found in the *Apostolic Constitutions*. These writings reflect the cumulative absorption into Judaism of elements from Orphism, eclectic Greek philosophy, the Isiac and Hermetic mysteries and Iranian thought. The Torah comes to be interpreted as a mystic revelation of the ladder of spiritual ascent "through the great Saviors, to the Light-Stream and its Source, true salvation."

The following quotations typify the promises of this emerging mystic Judaism:

> But look unto the Word Divine, and fix
> In Him your mind. Direct your heart
> To the intelligible sphere, tread well
> The Road; and have regard for Him alone
> Who is the immortal Framer of the world. . . . Though He
> Is ever present in His works, He yet
> Remains by mortal eyes unseen, By Nous
> Alone discerned. . . .[23]

> O ye foolish mortals, cease
> Roving in darkness and black night obscure,
> And leave the darkness of night, and lay hold
> Upon the Light.[24]

The divine Logos has ceaseless care over us, and teaches us both the passwords of our King and divine acts. O thou soul which hast been permeated with the power of the Logos! O trumpet of peace in the soul torn by conflict! O city of refuge from terrible passion! O teaching that quenches the fire within the soul! This instruction

---

21. S. H. Hooke, ed., *Myth and Ritual* (London, 1933); *The Labyrinth* (New York, 1935).
22. E. R. Goodenough, *By Light, Light* (New Haven, 1935), chaps. x, xi.
23. Aristobulus, in E. R. Goodenough, *op. cit.*, p. 280.
24. A fragment of a Sibylline oracle, cf. M. Terry, *The Sibylline Oracles* (New York, 1889), p. 259; E. R. Goodenough, *op. cit.*, pp. 284 f.

does not make us poets, it does not train us as philosophers, or as skilful orators, but when it has been learned, it makes mortals become immortals, human beings gods, and from earth leads to realms beyond Olympus.[25]

Probably the most important single witness to the Jewish development of this mystic gospel before the time of Philo is the Wisdom of Solomon. Here we find, according to Goodenough, "a definite and elaborate Mystery of Sophia, one that is certainly non-Philonic in origin, and . . . in all probability distinctly pre-Philonic in time."[26] By the time of this book, the age of conscious syncretism had passed, "the mystic and philosophic ideas of the Greek world have become completely naturalized within Judaism,"[27] and the writer was perfectly sincere in seeking for himself the goals of eclectic Hellenistic religion.

The process of fusion had not yet resulted in complete consistency or definite system, however, as is indicated by the presence of many contradictory ideas of reward in Wisdom. Here we find appeals to external material rewards during this life according to the theory of exact retribution, Chapters 16–18; external reward after death, Chapters 1–6; the attainment of the Stoic life of happiness, virtue and tranquillity; and the mystic participation in the Light-Stream through the gift of divine wisdom.[28]

The divine wisdom is in part the natural endowment of rational men and in part the result of the discipline of the will. The consequent rewards of this aspect of wisdom are consonant with the Stoic ideal.

> God created man for incorruption
> And made him an image of his own proper being [i.e., his rational selfhood];
> But by the envy of the devil death entered the world,
> And they that are of his portion make trial thereof.[29]

The supreme punishment of vices, the surrender to passions, is the death of the rational self and "the eternal deprivation of the vision of God." Cain, for example, perishes in the rage wherewith he slays his brother. Idolators and unreasoning men suffer from unceasing fears, hatred, confusion, ignorance, and mental agony.[30]

Those who achieve righteousness and virtue through obeying God attain complete freedom from care, grief, fear, and anxiety.

> The fruits of wisdom's labors are virtues;
> For she teacheth soberness and understanding, righteousness and courage
> And there is nothing in life for men more profitable than these.[31]

---

25. *Oratio ad Graecos*, 5. Cf. E. R. Goodenough, *op. cit.*, p. 300.
26. E. R. Goodenough, *op. cit.*, p. 276.
27. *Idem*, p. 297. Cf. also W. L. Knox, *St. Paul and the Church of the Gentiles* (Cambridge, 1939), chaps. ii, iii.
28. Wisdom 1.1–16; 2.20–24; 3.10–12; 4.1, 2, 7–16; 5.6–13; 6.1–12.11; 12.16–13.9; 15.1–18.4; 18.21–25.
29. *Idem*, 2.23 f.   30. *Idem*, 1.11; 10.2; 12.23–27; 14.21–31.
31. *Idem*, 8.7; 10.9; 16.8, 26.

Rewards in either the present age or the future life are inconsequential to those who have realized perfection of character in the present age.[32] Virtue is essentially timeless.

But wisdom is not simply the natural endowment which may be cultivated by self-discipline and literalistic law-observance. In its highest form it is a conferring of supernatural *gnosis* to one who has climbed the "mystic ladder" into direct mystical communion with God. The gift of wisdom reveals the true spiritual Law which for the mystic replaces the traditional literal Law as the guide to salvation. Wisdom is a clear effulgence of divine light, an unspotted mirror of God's goodness, imparting to men the gifts of prophecy, knowledge of holy things, power over the celestial forces, insight into the secrets of history and nature, and a deathless incorruptibility.[33] Here lies the special interest of the final editor; here, is the life that to him is life indeed.

In Philo, the outstanding genius of Dispersion Judaism during the first century, we reach a highly advanced stage in the fusion process. In him are joined many streams of influence: ancestral Judaism, the Pythagorean, Platonic and Stoic philosophical traditions, and the Oriental mysteries. The separate ideas are not adopted piecemeal, mechanically or consciously, but are inherited with the culture in which Philo was born.[34] Consequently, it is no easy matter to unravel the strands of his thought regarding the nature of rewards for righteousness.

Philo recognizes the need of using different inducements for different groups of people. All humanity is divided into two groups: men who recognize the value of virtue and men who do not. In the second group Philo places many of his fellow Jews who can obey the laws of goodness only through fear of incurring the wrath of God. In dealing with this group Philo admits the literal interpretation of the Torah with its consequent appeal to tangible historical rewards and punishments. But he definitely rejects this concept of salvation for himself and for all those who can appreciate the deeper, spiritual meaning of the divine wisdom.[35]

He is chiefly concerned with those who recognize the inherent values of virtue, and in his appeal to this group he proceeds throughout on the basic assumptions of Hellenistic philosophy. For example, he is completely in accord with Greek dualism. The soul of man, described variously as mind, reason, or spirit, is the image and copy of the eternal reason. The mind of man occupies the same relation to the body that God as Mind occupies to the world. The body of man is earthly and mortal; its passions are wholly irrational. Thus are

---

32. *Idem*, 4.7–14; 1.15; 8.18.
33. *Idem*, 6.18 f.; 7.16–22; 7.28 ff.; 9.1 ff.; 10.10–12. Cf. also Knox, *op. cit.*, pp. 57 f.
34. "For two centuries or more before Philo the Jews in Egypt . . . found in their environment that type of thought ready made which we can only describe by an extended hyphenization, a Persian-Isiac-Platonic-Pythagorean mystery." E. R. Goodenough, *op. cit.*, p. 237.
35. Philo, *Leg. Alleg.* 1.93–4; *Quod Deus Imm.* 60–69.

preserved both the Stoic antithesis of reason vs. passion and the Platonic, Pythagorean, and Mystery antithesis of mind vs. body.[36]

As corollary of this idea, Philo rejects external sanctions such as length of life, wealth, health, honor, because they are made of "perishable stuff," and finds the locus of value in the health of the soul.[37] A second corollary is belief in the immortality of the rational divine nature of man. This immortality is dissociated from any thought of future retribution, physical resurrection or apocalyptic consummation of history. It is the receiving of an incorruptible soul entirely freed from limitations of space and time. There is no death to the spiritual life except that which comes as a result of sin.

The ultimate sanction is the promise of happiness, which dwells "not in anything external, or in things connected with the body, or even in every part of the soul, but in the sovereign principle alone; for the mind, the temple of God, bears the good as a divine image."[38] The acquisition of salvation involves the development of the "sovereign principle" and this is possible only through the "practice of perfect virtue in a perfect life."[39] And this life of perfect virtue includes for Philo all the values sought by the Stoic sages: freedom from the passions,[40] complete tranquillity and self-control, acceptance of external fortunes,[41] harmony with natural law.

The story of the Jewish heroes is allegorized to represent the fulfilment of this gospel of salvation. The reward of Abraham's virtue was faith:

Faith toward God is the only undeceiving and certain good, the consolation of life, the fulness of good hopes, the banishment of evils, the bringing of blessings, the renunciation of misfortunes, the knowledge of piety, the possession of happiness, the bettering in all things of the soul which rests for its support upon Him who is the cause of all things, and who, though He can do all things, wills only to do what is best.[42]

Isaac's reward was complete joy: "He is free from all depression and melancholy, and as he enjoys a life exempt from sorrow and exempt from fear, hav-

---

36. Philo, *De Opif. Mund.* 23 f.; *Leg. Alleg.* 3.161; *De Migr. Abr.* 9; *Quod Det. Pot.* 82–90; *De Virtut.* 188.

37. Philo, *Post. Cain* 112–115; *De Gig.* 34–38; *Quod Deus Imm.* 150 f.; T. H. Billings, *Platonism of Philo Judaeus* (Chicago, 1919), pp. 77 f.

38. James Drummond, *Philo* (London, 1888), II, 285 f.; Philo, *Post. Cain* 39; *Leg. Alleg.* 1.97 f.; 3.167 f.; 3.217 ff.; 3.245 ff.; *De Agric.* 25; *De Praem.* 2 f. Cf. also T. H. Billings, *op. cit.*, p. 72.

39. Philo, *Quod Det. Pot.* 57–60; *De Mutat. Nom.* 41; *De Praem.* 14; *De Ebriet.* 6–10; *Leg. Alleg.* 3.245 f.; *Quod Deus Imm.* 154; *De Agric.* 157; *Sac. of Cain* 33 f.; *De Spec. Leg.* II, 259.

40. Philo, *De Cher.* 96; *Leg. Alleg.* 3.3, 19, 33, 249; 2.106–108; *Post. Cain* 22, 183, 184; *Sac. of Cain* 49 f.; *De Praem.* 12; *Quis Rer. Div.* 106 ff.

41. Philo, *Quod Det. Pot.* 51 f.; *De Plant.* 49 ff.; *Quis Rer. Div.* 95 f.; *De Spec. Leg.* 1.202 f.; 3.48 f.; N. Bentwich, *op. cit.*, pp. 186 f.; E. R. Goodenough, *op. cit.*, pp. 389 f.

42. Philo, *De Abr.* 268, 263 f.; *De Praem.* 27 f.; *Quis Rer. Div.* 91; *De Cherub.* 85; *De Migr. Abr.* 44.

ing no connection, not even in a dream, with any painful or austere plans of life, because every part of his soul is wholly occupied with joy."[43]

But while the patriarchs are extolled as receiving the typically Stoic rewards for the development of the natural immanent reason, they had much deeper significance for Philo. They were revealers of the way in which the divine Mind is imparted to select initiates, a wisdom that is conferred through divine grace rather than through human attainment. They revealed through the Law the "royal road" to the highest mystical union with God. Having themselves climbed the steep ascent, they were now the hierophants of the Jewish mystery by whose help others might mount.

The supreme quality in Philo's ideal of happiness is the fulfilment of this mystic quest for direct vision of God and union with Him. The Stoic program may prepare the way for this supreme gift, but the gift itself is more akin to the salvation offered in the mysteries.

Seeing then that our souls are a region open to His invisible entrance, let us make that place as beautiful as we may, to be a lodging fit for God. Else He will pass silently into some other home, where He judges that the builder's hands have wrought something worthier. . . .

One house worthy there is—the soul that is fitted to receive Him. . . . And that the house may have both strength and loveliness, let its foundation be laid in natural excellence and good teaching, and let us rear upon them virtues and noble actions, and let its external ornaments be the reception of the learning of the schools. . . .

If such a house be raised . . ., earth and all that dwells on earth will be filled with high hopes, expecting the descent of the divine potencies. With laws and ordinances from heaven they will descend, to sanctify and consecrate them on earth.[44]

When these "divine potencies" descend, the individual soul is lifted out of all contact with its bodily prison, the world, and the events of ordinary life. The soul leaves the self, all time ceases, the steady contemplation of God emerges in the direct unmediated apprehension of divine Truth, the invasion of a divine effulgence and the exhilaration of overflowing joy. The soul is absorbed in a glorious vision in which the whole universe with all its secrets opens as a book, is enveloped in a warm radiance, and is gripped by a prophetic frenzy.[45]

Among those who seek this experience, Philo recognized three groups: those who have just started, those who are progressing toward the goal, and those who have achieved or received perfection. Each step requires appropriate

---

43. Philo, *De Praem.* 4–8; *De Fuga* 176; *De Plant.* 168; *De Ebriet.* 62; *De Spec. Leg.* 2.48–55.

44. Philo, *De Cherub.* 100–106. For the fullest description of this aspect of Philo's religion, cf. E. R. Goodenough, *op. cit.*, chaps. iv–ix.

45. Cf. W. L. Knox, *op. cit.*, chaps. ii–iii; Philo, *De Spec. Leg.* 1.36; *Quis Rer. Div.* 52 f., 265 f., 69 f.; *Leg. Alleg.* 1.82 f.; 3.44; *Vita Mos.* 3; *Justit.* 8; *De Praem.* 9; *Quaest. et Sol.* 3.9 f.; *De Mut. Nom.* 82; *De Abr.* 58; E. Bevan, *op. cit.*, pp. 45 ff.; H. R. Willoughby, *op. cit.*, pp. 247 ff.; H. A. A. Kennedy, *Philo's Contribution to Religion* (New York, 1919), chaps. vi–vii.

discipline. Men must first of all realize their own weakness and acknowledge their dependence upon God; they must separate themselves from their bodily prison by purifying themselves in rejecting the passions; they must renounce all fears, folly and worldly desires; they must put complete confidence in the world of the spirit; they must practice religious contemplation following the example of the Jewish patriarchs and seeking their help.[46] To a few only who take the road is the vision of God vouchsafed; but to all who try, sufficient reward is given.[47] There may be exaggeration, but there is truth in Professor Goodenough's characterization of Philo's religion as "a Judaism so thoroughly paganized that its postulates and its objectives were those of Hellenistic mysteries rather than those of any Judaism we have hitherto known. For all its passionate Jewish loyalty, it was not fundamentally a Judaism with Hellenistic veneer; it was a Hellenism presented in Jewish symbols and allegories, to be sure, but still a Hellenistic dream of the solution of the problem of life by ascent higher and ever higher in the streaming Light-Life of God."[48] Philo leaves his testimony to his own experience of this supreme happiness—redemption from the material world and its passions, a deep emotional ecstasy of mystic vision and union with God which he felt came only through divine grace. And there is less in common between his gospel of salvation and that of "normative" Judaism than there is between his view and that of the mystery religions.

C. The Success of Syncretism.

The positive contribution of Philo and other Jewish syncretists was not unimportant. Placed in critical political, economic and racial situations, they remained loyal to their God and His revealed Law all the while they adjusted their faith to meet the demands of their day. Appreciating the validity of Gentile quests for redemption they affirmed that their true fulfilment was possible only through obedience to the divine source of truth and virtue. In their efforts at adjustment, however, they came no nearer to an enduring solution of the problem of reward. Progressively they surrender faith in the Jewish hope of social redemption within the historical process, the assurance of concrete retribution in the total sphere of man's life, the confidence in the justice and mercy of God as undergirding every historical event. No typical Jewish idea of salvation survives the adoption of Hellenistic standards of value. To be sure, the liabilities of the Jewish pattern disappear with the assets. Philo and the others can hardly be charged with egoistic prudentialism, economic lust for power, materialistic secularism, or particularistic nationalism. On the other hand, every distinctively Hellenistic sanction appears in increasing strength:

---

46. Philo, *Leg. Alleg.* 3.41; *Quod Det. Pot.* 158 f.; *De Praem.* 26; *Quis Rer. Div.* 69 f., 249 ff.; *De Somn.* 1.148, 236; *De Gig.* 54; *De Post. Cain* 31.
47. Philo, *De Post. Cain* 21; *De Spec. Leg.* 1.36; *De Plant.* 37; *Leg. Alleg.* 3.48.
48. E. R. Goodenough, *op. cit.*, p. 264.

the promises of freedom from carnality and passion, from external compulsions and misfortunes, of a peaceful conscience in harmony with the universal-personal laws of reason, of self-control and virtuous happiness, and of the regeneration of the spirit of man by the reception of *gnosis*, vision, and incorruptible divine Light and Life.

The prophetic character of Judaism conditions the use of these sanctions by a continued insistence upon the transcendence of God, the interpretation of God's demands in moral terms, and the rejection of amoral mysticism, magical sacramentarianism and orgiastic emotionalism. But the crucial fallacies of Gentile conceptions of happiness are not evaded: the extreme dualistic metaphysics and psychology, the resultant spiritualism, individualism, subjectivism and relativism. The age-old problem of unfulfilled expectations, the recurrent frustrations of suffering saints, is met in a thoroughly un-Jewish fashion by the denial of meaning to history, indifference to social redemption, segmentation of man's life, and restriction of God's saving activity to the realm above history.

This is the crux of the matter: can a religion that is based on faith in a historically active and righteous personal God, who has sealed an everlasting covenant with his people, solve the dilemma of historical frustrations without surrendering its distinctive philosophy of history, its understanding of society, and its secular hope? We have seen that Jewish apocalypticism was the most profound attempt by Palestinian Jews to reconcile the contradictions of experience with faith in the divine meaning and goal of history. We have also seen that Hellenistic Judaism, inoculated against the virus of apocalypticism by the sophisticated rationalism of Gentile culture, surrendered the prophetic faith in history in adopting the Hellenistic goals of religion. Neither the apocalyptic nor the syncretistic answers to the problem are wholly satisfactory; each is fragmentary and vulnerable. The question emerges in this form: did Jewish apocalypticism when transferred to the Gentile environment achieve a more satisfactory synthesis than Jewish legalism? And if so, how? To answer these questions we must analyze the philosophy of salvation of emerging Christianity, for the gospel which Jesus preached represents the flowering of Jewish apocalypticism and the gospel of the Christian missionaries represents a unique attempt to accommodate that apocalyptic gospel to the needs of the Gentile world.

CHAPTER IV

The Gospel of Jesus

A. The Environment of Jesus.

IN approaching the work of Jesus we return to the genuinely Jewish milieu, in which the expectation of rewards followed different patterns and was subject to different challenges. Jesus was born a Jew and spent his life in Palestinian surroundings. He was a lineal spiritual descendant of the prophets, psalmists and apocalyptists. To be sure, Hellenistic culture had invaded his homeland, but Jewish cultural influences, though on the defensive, were still dominant in the circles in which he moved. In fact, the infiltration of pagan institutions, ideals, and economy accentuated the tensions with which Jesus' message came to grips. For Jesus' contemporaries were faced with a deep-seated cultural crisis which forms the backdrop for his work.

Imperialism and commercialism were twin devils harrying the Jews. Roman soldiers and governors rode roughshod over their customs and liberties. Exorbitant taxes were imposed by the rulers irrespective of the religious tithes, taxes which rested most heavily upon the poorer classes and which totaled as much as forty to fifty per cent of the total income. The currency was controlled by aliens. Farms were foreclosed by Gentile land-sharks so that property became concentrated in the hands of a few absentee landowners, whose stewards controlled the estates and sublet sections to share-croppers. An agricultural economy, able in good years to support the native population, became unable to provide both security for the homeland and profits for the foreign exploiters. Security came to depend more upon the world commercial economy than upon the fertility of the Jewish homeland. The chief purpose of the Roman garrisons was to preserve the financial interests of the foreign traders, and to this end emperor worship served as a cultural tool. Roman imperialism thus provoked an aggressive nationalism among loyal Jews, as evidenced by: refusal to use coins engraved with the emperor's image, hatred of publicans and "puppet rulers," tax strikes, boycotts of alien commerce, the formation of armed guerilla bands, and subterranean boiling of apocalyptic hopes in anticipation of a volcanic eruption. Religious leaders were forced to give some answer to the question: "Is it right to give tribute to Caesar?"[1]

This political unrest was in part an expression of economic distress. There is evidence in the gospels of many of these sources of struggle: unemployment,

---

1. Cf. Josephus, *Antiquities*, 17.6.2; 17.8.4; 17.11.2, 4; 18.1.1 f.; 18.3.2; F. C. Grant, *Economic Background of the Gospels* (London, 1926), pp. 46–54; W. Bousset, *Jesus* (New York, 1906), pp. 71 ff.; V. G. Simkhovitch, *Toward an Understanding of Jesus* (New York, 1925), pp. 34 f. An excellent fictional portrayal of conditions is found in S. Asch, *The Nazarene* (New York, 1939).

foreclosure of mortgages, the selling into slavery for debt, insecurity of widows and orphans, unscrupulous trade practices. The older self-contained agricultural economy was disintegrating under the impacts of alien commerce, politics, and culture; strife multiplied between city and country, the commercial and the agricultural, the large and small landowners, Jew and Gentile, and among various factions of Jews. And Jesus was sensitive to the human cost of these conditions: the hopelessness of the beggars, the poverty of widows, the insecurity of workers, the devastation caused by demons, the suffering and fears of the poor, and the frustrations of the unchurched. Economic distress constituted one of the roots of the religious movement which came to focus all hopes upon the coming of an era in which prosperity, equality and security would be established. Each religious leader was forced to relate his faith to this immediate need for daily bread and for a brighter future.[2]

To Jews each source of political and economic unrest was at the same time a challenge to their unique faith in God and in his promises. The worship of Caesar was not merely acceptance of political domination; it was blasphemy. Each inch of cultural penetration made it impossible for more Jews to be true to their heritage. Participation in commerce with a Gentile wine-merchant violated the Torah. They could not compete with other merchants without breaking the Sabbath or polluting themselves. They could not walk to the temple in Jerusalem without passing the amphitheater, the stadium, or the market place. Loyalty to the Jewish Torah multiplied the restraints of trade against the loyalists; they were forced either to adopt unscrupulous economic practices or face gradual economic extinction. No religious movement could escape this question: How can I become righteous according to the dictates of the Law without falling into the debtors' prison and the life of slavery? How can those who have unwillingly become unclean sinners ever hope to receive the salvation of God? Not only was this a crisis in the life of the loyal Jew, it was a challenge to the ultimate truth of the Jewish faith. Is God really in control of history? Is his kingdom an idle fantasy? When will he save his people? Experience undermined their faith, but they could not surrender their faith without surrendering their sole clue to the moral meaning and purpose of history.

The basic antithesis confronting the Jewish people was the decision for or against the existing conditions. At one extreme the Sadducees made their peace with the present. They were the priestly aristocracy, a wealthy minority whose security was assured by gentlemen's agreements with the Roman overlords. They were hospitable to alien customs, protesting against too rigorous observance of Jewish traditions, frowning upon popular discontent. Their religion became a tool of class interest, used to maintain their pride and prestige and

---

2. Cf. F. C. Grant, *op. cit.*, pp. 64–68, 112 f.; M. Dibelius, *Der Brief des Jakobus* (Gottingen, 1921), pp. 37–44; *Johannes dem Taufer* (Gottingen, 1911), 129 ff.; Josephus, *Antiquities*, 15.7.10; 17.6.1 f.; 17.8.1 f.; 17.11.1–5. Evidence of the economic conditions permeates the gospels. Cf. Matthew 18.23–35; 20.1–16; 21.33–46; 25.14–30; Luke 6.20–26; 7.41; 12.13–21; 16.1–13, 19–31; 19.1–27; 21.1–4.

the status quo. For them the way was clear to harmonize the teachings of the scriptures with Greek philosophy.

At the extreme left were the Zealots, whose enmity with the existing order led them into violent rebellion against the alien rulers and against all manifestations of heathenism. Politically, they were following an impossible dream; their efforts could only provoke bloody reprisals and deepen their serfdom. Economically, their struggle could only weaken the people whom they sought to save. Religiously, they oversimplified the crisis by attributing all evil to political causes and by assuming that political freedom would guarantee religious reformation.

A third answer to the problem was offered by the Pharisees who persistently attempted to avoid pollution through contact with Hellenistic culture. Doggedly they tried to include the whole scope of their lives within the purview of inherited faith; loyally they preserved and enriched the Law and tradition. They wished to restore the true Israel through renewed, painstaking observance of the Law. But this forced them to renounce political aspirations and to separate themselves from the common people for whom ritual purity was impossible. "Prophetic in theology, legalistic in ethics," they tried to recapture the true faith by looking toward the past, but they failed to come to direct grips with the national and social crisis of the present. As Professor Dibelius has said:

The Pharisees did not produce a distinctive eschatology. And that is easily understood: where the Law, the regulation of existing relationships, is the "hot-spot" of all religious living, there must the future hope retire into the background, because the hearts of the righteous belong to the existing age and not to the coming age.[3]

Professor Vlastos has pointed out the way in which Pharisaism was in effect a defence of the established order rather than a realistic protest against it.[4]

A solution of the problem more truly in harmony with the genius of prophetic Judaism is found in eschatology. Professor Dibelius has thus outlined the social ground for this answer:

Eschatological expectations were more vital and richer, . . . in the unliterary masses, in the so called *Amhaarez*, in those circles in which the present was experienced as hopeless, and who must look to the future for everything they desired. Here lay the sphere of influence for the coming religious reformation. Neither in the circles which had concluded friendship with the Hellenistic world and for whom this friendship brought peace, nor in the circles to whom the Law provided everything they needed: an other-worldly revelation and a minute regulation of conduct, could such a reformation be established. To those who were satisfied on both counts, Jesus and John had nothing to give. Their message could only find receptive hearers where religious faith was still full of tension, where piety was still an unsatisfied

---

3. M. Dibelius, *Johannes dem Taufer*, p. 130.
4. G. Vlastos, "Jesus' Conflict with the Pharisees," *Christendom*, II (1937), 86 f.

The Gospel of Jesus

longing, where the Greek view of the body had not been felt, and where the instruction in the Law had not silenced all questions and desires of the heart. Whoever would bring a new religious impulse could not be a philosopher or a scribe, but must be a man of the people.[5]

With this understanding of the environment in which Jesus' message took form, with this conviction that apocalyptic eschatology was a vital and valid religious expression of the faith and hope of the oppressed and dispossessed, we turn to the analysis of Jesus' message of salvation.

B. The Fundamentals of Jesus' Religion.

While our special concern is for the element of reward in the teaching of Jesus, we cannot ignore the basic structure of his thought. The ultimate authority and ground of faith lay for him in the will of God. He was intensely loyal to God, and the conviction of God's reality, his historical activity, and his justice and mercy dominated his life. For him the divine will was absolutely supreme. This will is revealed authoritatively in the scriptures. He may have differed with the scribes on the importance and interpretation and validity of certain prescriptions, but he "recognized absolutely a nucleus of the Torah as the revealed will of God and did not alter the fundamental character of the Jewish religion as an ethic of obedience."[6]

In his thought concerning man Jesus assumed the typical Jewish psychological monism: man is an inseparable unity of body and soul. Salvation is salvation of man's whole life, not of a segment. Likewise, Jesus assumed the corporate basis of the divine covenant; he is everywhere closer to Jewish collectivism than to Hellenistic individualism. The fulfilment of God's covenant would affect the social and historical life of men, of persons-in-community.

As a corollary of these structural beliefs, Jesus shared the Jewish faith in retribution on the plane of historical, communal existence. As God determines destiny, the destinies of the whole man and the whole of society, in accordance with his justice and mercy as revealed in the demands and promises of the covenant, so also he rewards all obedience and punishes all apostasy.

We have seen the challenge which continuing Jewish experience gave to this faith, and we have seen that in the apocalyptic tradition the challenge to faith is met by a progressive postponement of divine retribution from the present age to the coming kingdom. Jesus stood with the authors of Second Enoch and the Assumption of Moses as representative of the final stage in this de-

---

5. M. Dibelius, *op. cit.*, pp. 130–131; C. C. McCown, *Genesis of the Social Gospel*, pp. 286 ff.; C. C. McCown, "The Great Apostasy," *Christendom*, I (1936), 792 f.

6. H. Windisch, *Der Sinn der Bergpredigt* (Leipzig, 1929), p. 72; cf. also, B. W. Bacon, *Studies in Matthew* (New York, 1930), p. 357; G. F. Moore, *Judaism*, I, 269 f.; II, 9 f.; B. H. Branscomb, *Jesus and the Law of Moses* (New York, 1930), pp. 113–125; C. Guignebert, *Jesus* (New York, 1935), pp. 297 f.; A. N. Wilder, *Eschatology and Ethics in the Teaching of Jesus* (New York, 1939), pp. 147 f.

velopment. His belief was that divine salvation is not mediated during the present age; God now treats good and evil men alike.[7] Suffering is not an index of sin. The restoration of justice awaits the Judgment Day and the messianic era.

Here we should pause to outline Jesus' expectations concerning that kingdom. There is not time for qualifying carefully the description of Jesus' outlook or for submitting evidence to support it. The reader is referred to more complete treatments of Jesus' apocalypticism.[8] Jesus anticipated the coming of a new age in which God's will would be done "on earth as it is in heaven," a state of affairs rather than a state of mind.[9] The coming of this kingdom was still in the future; its consummation awaited social and cosmic upheavals and the inauguration of the Judgment Day.[10] The transition from this age to the next was believed to be immediately at hand.[11] It would come suddenly, without advance "signs," as a miracle of divine activity in history.[12] The decisive struggle between God and Satan was under way; certain strategic victories had already been won by God on the heavenly plane; the world process was moving toward its crisis, and the mystery of the divine operation had been revealed.[13] In fact, certain powers of the arriving kingdom were already effective and observable in the message and mission of Jesus, in his authority, his exorcism of demons, and in the prophetic activity of Jesus and his disciples.[14] These present anticipations of coming events made certain their consummation during that very generation. Men were confronted with the necessity of decision: contentment with life in the present age and its rewards or complete devotion to the demands of the kingdom and concentrated hope for its rewards. We turn, then, to an analysis of these rewards and their significance for the total message of Jesus to his contemporaries.

C. Reward in the Religion of Jesus.

In previous Jewish apocalypses, the character of the social-religious crisis conditioned the character of rewards. When the primary crisis had been na-

---

7. Matthew 5.45; Luke 13.2–5.
8. Cf. Rudolph Otto, *The Kingdom of God and Son of Man* (Grand Rapids, n.d.); A. N. Wilder, *op. cit.*; E. F. Scott, *The Kingdom and the Messiah* (Edinburgh, 1911); C. Guignebert, *op. cit.*, pp. 325 ff.; R. N. Flew, *Jesus and His Church* (New York, 1938), chaps. i–iii; T. W. Manson, *Teaching of Jesus* (Cambridge, 1931), chaps. vi–viii.
9. Mark 10.28–31; 14.57–59; Matthew 6.10; Luke 22.18; 12.32.
10. Mark 13.7–12, 14–20, 24–27; 8.38; Matthew 22.1 f.; 12.36; Luke 6.20 f., 43 f.; 10.13–15; 11.29–32; 17.34 f.
11. Mark 1.14; 9.1; 13.28–30; Matthew 10.23; Luke 10.11; 11.51; 17.20 f.
12. Mark 13.33–37; 8.12; Luke 11.29–32; 12.32–38; 17.20 f.; 18.1–8.
13. Mark 3.27; Luke 10.17–20, 23–24; 11.20; 16.16; Matthew 11.25 ff. Cf. A. N. Wilder, *op. cit.*, pp. 34–41; Johannes Weiss, *History of Primitive Christianity* (New York, 1937), pp. 519 f.
14. Mark 2.28; 4.1–9, 30–32; 9.11–13; Luke 7.18–23; 11.29–32; 10.22. A. N. Wilder, *op. cit.*, chap. viii.

tional defeat and oppression, the religious hope anticipated the imminent overthrow of the enemy and the inception of a period of national freedom and prosperity. In crises produced by the individual martyrdom of loyalists, religious thought tended to envisage their resurrection. In periods of bitter internecine strife between rich Jews and poor Jews, prophets foresaw the sudden and complete reversal of fortunes of these two groups within Israel. Jesus was not deeply influenced by the need for political independence and national freedom, refusing to take any part in irredentist agitation during his lifetime. He seems to have been most sensitive to the economic and social injustices within Judaism, the suffering of the righteous poor; consequently, his ideas of the future kingdom include the expectation of imminent reversal of the social and economic pyramid.

> Blessed are ye poor, for yours is the kingdom of God. . . .
> Woe to ye rich, for ye have received your reward. . . .

The last will be first, and the first last; the humble will be exalted, and the proud humbled; the poor will rejoice and the rich lament. Tidings of the new era are "good news" to the disinherited loyalists.[15]

While there are symbolic and mythological elements in Jesus' pictures of the kingdom, they represent more than symbols or myths. The blessings of the kingdom would be tangible and concrete, even though Jesus did not attempt their literal description. He simply uses current metaphors to suggest the desirability of life in the new age: the metaphors of the feast, the wedding, the twelve thrones, the harvest.

The forms taken by this expectation were no accident; one of the surest of psychological laws, the very one that governs all dreams of the hungry and persecuted . . . —the prisoner's dream of deliverance, the fever-stricken man's vision of cooling waters, the famine sufferer's dream of bread . . . rendered inevitable their choice of imagery.[16]

The chief rewards to which Jesus appealed are all eschatological: acquittal in the judgment, entrance into the kingdom, the inheritance of life therein and all its treasures. The penalties are sufferings in Gehenna and exclusion from the life of the coming age. A close analysis of the teaching materials in the gospels reveals about ninety separate units, in more than two-thirds of which may be found the expectation of rewards and punishments in the coming kingdom.[17] Professor Wilder in an independent study has corroborated this con-

---

15. Mark 8.35; 10.31; Luke 9.24; 17.33; 13.22–30; 14.16–24; 16.19–31; 18.14; Matthew 10.39; 16.25; 14.27–30; 20.16. With the Lucan beatitudes and woes, cf. II Enoch 9; 51.3; 66.6; 52.1–15; I Enoch 94.8; 96.5–8; 98.13.
16. F. C. Grant, *op. cit.*, p. 107; C. C. McCown, *op. cit.*, pp. 286 f.; A. N. Wilder, *op. cit.*, chap. iii.
17. Numbered according to A. Huck, *Synopse der drei ersten Evangelien* (seventh edition, Tubin-

clusion.[18] Let us review some of these teachings, moving from the less ambiguous to the more ambiguous passages.

Among the least ambiguous is Jesus' teaching on hospitality.

When thou makest a dinner or a supper, call not thy friends, nor thy brethren, nor thy kinsmen, nor rich neighbors, lest haply they also bid thee again, and a recompense be made thee. But when thou makest a feast, bid the poor, the maimed, the lame, the blind: and thou shalt be blessed, because they have not wherewith to recompense thee; for thou shalt be recompensed in the resurrection of the just.[19]

Clearly, Jesus was primarily more interested in righteousness than in prudence, but he appeals frankly to men's desire for reward in the coming age. The same appeal is explicit in the exhortations to liberal almsgiving. Generosity stores up treasures in heaven. For men who use their alms as a means of getting earthly honor the present glory is sufficient recompense; but for men who give freely in secret the compensation is glory and wealth in the kingdom.[20] This requirement of present sacrifice for inheritance of the kingdom is placed upon the rich ruler.[21] It constitutes also the point of the story of Zacchaeus, the parable of the rich fool, and the parable of Dives. "Remember that you received your good things in your life time, and Lazarus received evil things; but now here he is comforted, but you are tormented."[22] The implied advice to all is the same: "Sell your possessions and give alms" and the implied sanction is the same: "And you shall have treasure in heaven." For all these special cases the general principle holds: "It is easier for a camel to go through a needle's eye than for a rich man to enter the kingdom of heaven."[23] To retain wealth is the service of the present age, the kingdom of Mammon and of Satan. To accept voluntary poverty by giving alms is the service of God and his kingdom. No compromise between the two is possible.

The teachings of the rabbis offer parallels to this cycle of ideas.

Truly a good man, say the Rabbis, was King Munhaz. During a famine he gave to the poor the treasury of his father. His relations upbraided him: what thy father saved thou hast thrown away. Munhaz answered: My father laid up treasure on earth; I gather it in the heavens. My father hoarded it where hands might steal; I placed it beyond the reach of human hands. My father saved money; I have saved life.... My father saved for this world; I save for the next.[24]

gen, 1928), the units implying the expectation of reward in the kingdom are as follows: 19, 21, 22, 26–32, 35, 36, 40, 42, 43, 46, 58, 60, 62, 63, 66, 74, 86–88, 96, 100–102, 115, 123, 129, 131, 136, 154, 161, 167, 169, 170, 174, 177, 184, 185, 187–190, 192, 194, 195, 204, 205, 208, 215, 216, 219, 222, 225, 226, 227, 229. In some of these cases the reference to future recompense betrays the outlook of the early church rather than Jesus (e.g., 63, 100, 102, 170, 195, 204, 215, 229), but this number is balanced by the cases in which several distinct appeals to future awards appear in a single unit (e.g., 19, 189).

18. A. N. Wilder, *op. cit.*, chaps. iv, v.
19. Luke 14.12–14.
20. Matthew 6.2–4, 19–21; Luke 6.24–26; 12.33 f.
21. Mark 10.17–25.
22. Luke 16.25; 19.1–10; 12.16–21.
23. Mark 10.25.
24. Cf. A. Plummer, *Matthew* (London, 1909), p. 106; also G. Dalman, *Jesus-Jeshua* (New York, 1929), p. 65.

Similar examples of Jesus' thought are found in his teachings on forgiveness. "For if you forgive men their trespasses, your heavenly Father will also forgive you. But if you forgive not men their trespasses neither will your Father forgive your trespasses."[25] Here, too, Jesus speaks for the Jewish tradition, which follows a closely knit chain of development from the wisdom literature of the Old Testament through Sirach to the rabbis. Future forgiveness for present forbearance is the point of the parable of the unforgiving steward.[26]

The principle of retribution is further summarized in the thoroughly Jewish proverb: "With what measure ye mete, it shall be measured unto you again." In Matthew this proverb is used as a deterrent from personal criticism and condemnation: "Judge not that ye be not judged."[27] In Luke it is used to support obedience to four different types of behavior: "Judge not, and ye shall not be judged; Condemn not, and ye shall not be condemned; Release, and ye shall be released; Give, and it shall be given unto you."[28]

Jesus makes clear the belief that when one loves those who love him, he will receive no future reward, for the balance is even. Likewise there will be no future recompense for the man who does good to those who treat him well, or for the man who collects the loans he has made. One should love, treat kindly, and lend money, hoping for no just return during this age.[29]

Consider the large group of eschatological axioms, scattered through the teaching tradition, which preserve this outlook.

> Whosoever saves his life shall lose it,
> And whosoever loses his life . . . shall save it.[30]
>
> The last shall be first, and the first last.[31]
>
> Whosoever exalts himself shall be humbled,
> Whosoever humbles himself shall be exalted.[32]
>
> Whosoever would be first of all and greatest of all,
> Let him be last of all and servant of all.[33]

These proverbs converge into one general principle. Many who are last, who voluntarily hold the humblest stations accepting a life of unrequited service, will be received with distinction into the messianic kingdom.

There is danger lest moderns judge such a frank appeal to self-regarding

---

25. Matthew 6.11–15; Mark 11.24, 25; Luke 11.4; compare Sirach 28.2; II Enoch 1.4; T.Z. 5.3; 8.2; T.G. 6.3–7; T.I. 5.2; G. Dalman, *op. cit.*, p. 226.
26. Matthew 18.34–35; Luke 16.5–9.   27. Matthew 7.1 f.
28. Luke 6.37, 38.   29. *Idem*, 6.27–35.
30. Mark 8.35; Luke 9.24; 17.33; Matthew 10.39; 16.35. Cf. C. G. Montefiore, *Synoptic Gospels* (London, 1909), I, 206; A. E. J. Rawlinson, *St. Mark* (London, 1925), on Mark 8.35.
31. Mark 10.28–31; Matthew 19.27–30; 20.16; Luke 13.22–30. Cf. also C. G. Montefiore, *op. cit.*, I, 254.
32. Matthew 23.12; Luke 14.11; 18.14.   33. Mark 9.35; 10.44 and parallels.

motives as a crass example of egoistic utilitarianism. This danger is lessened for those who approach Jesus from the standpoint of prophetic Judaism, and who realize that Jesus was a prophet who was primarily concerned with the autonomous demands of God for humility, sacrifice and service, and who was dealing directly with loyal Jews whose sufferings placed a great strain upon their faith. Both Jesus and the prophets used eudaemonism as ". . . their great moral lever. As historians and in direct sermons they pointed the lesson of rewards and punishments. The result of good and evil doing is not mentioned merely as an observed fact; it is unblushingly appealed to as a motive."[34]

From first to last Jesus was an eschatological prophet to whom imminent historical events heightened the divine demand for repentance and obedience. This demand was the prior condition and sole ground for any hope of salvation. All the separate teachings of Jesus concerning the need for storing up treasures in heaven are concentrated in the call to repentance. Soon the kingdom would appear in its fulness "as a lightning flash across the sky," similar in its catastrophic suddenness to the flood and the destruction of Sodom. There would be no time for further preparation. All men would be divided into two groups and either rejected or admitted. To avert the threatened destruction and to inherit the promised salvation, repentance was necessary. Jesus proclaimed this demand in trenchant tones, reminding his hearers of those who had been killed by calamities in their own cities: "If you do not repent, all of you shall likewise perish." Israel was pictured as the unproductive fig tree, given one more chance to bear fruit before its destruction.[35]

The basic teaching concerning repentance illustrates the relation of two elements in Jesus' message: the frank appeal to eschatological rewards and penalties, and the uncompromising demand for moral revolution.

For him it [repentance] is not negative but positive, not compartmentalized but totalitarian, not oriented toward the past and distant future but grounded in the present and the immediate future. It is a dynamic quality of life which consistently and continually interprets one's whole life—personal and social, conscious and unconscious, assumptions and actions—in the light of a moral reality that transcends self, that makes ultimate moral demands upon one. It is the shift in the very center of life that results from a viewing of the present in the light of the eternal, a seeing of the self from the perspective of the divine. It is continuing, rigorous and creative self-criticism in the light of God's will, a radical revolution in man's life that originates in the confrontation of the righteousness of God and the claims of his kingdom.[36]

For Jesus, the center of life is God, the ultimate imperative is to love God, the ultimate standard is the will of God, and the ultimate hope is the kingdom

---

34. H. J. Cadbury, "Jesus and the Prophets," *Journal of Religion*, V (1925), 619 ff.; *The Peril of Modernizing Jesus* (New York, 1937), pp. 101–111.
35. Luke 13.3, 5; also 17.22–29; Matthew 10.25; 11.20–23; 12.41; 16.4; 24.37–41.
36. P. S. Minear, "Repentance," *Religion in Life*, VII (1938), 578.

of God, which will be God's supreme gift to his covenant people. The consequent promises of dawn and threats of doom are derived from his faith, not the efficient cause of that faith. Man's desire for salvation is valid, but is dependent upon the divine purpose. Man may pray "Thy kingdom come," but not simply in order to conserve his own interests; rather in order that God's will may be done on earth as in heaven. The love of God and obedience to him constitute the first imperative. For Jesus as for the prophets before him, the *Law* is the necessary basis for the *Promise,* and obedience is the sole ground of hope. Man's desire for life and his dependence upon God's purpose are epitomized in the paradox "He that saveth his life shall lose it, and he that loseth his life shall save it." The same paradox is illustrated in the prayer attributed to Jesus in Gethsemane. The motive of loving God includes but transcends the motive of seeking life in the kingdom.

This emphasis distinguished Jesus' message from that of many apocalyptists. Their writings had largely served the purposes of consolation and compensation for those who believed themselves to be righteous, in order to buttress their faith against untoward circumstances. The message of approaching judgment had not been directed toward winning back the wicked from apostasy or toward challenging the accepted standards of righteousness of the loyalists. Rewards offered were largely in the form of compensations for sacrifices and losses already suffered. For Jesus, the anticipation of God's kingdom became the basis for a fervent appeal to repentance, for reclaiming men who would otherwise have been lost, for demanding greater sacrifices still to be made. To him, God's will implied a condemnation of contemporary norms of righteousness and the substitution of an absolute standard. He called men voluntarily to accept injustice "for righteousness' sake" as a preparation for life in the kingdom. Consequently, he was not so concerned with speculation as to the date and signs of the kingdom's approach, as if man's hope depended simply upon those external events, but he spent his energies preparing men morally who were now unprepared. Men must seek the kingdom of God *and His righteousness.* He found that his message of repentance was more readily received by those who knew themselves to be sinners than by those who trusted in their righteousness.

This dependence of apocalyptic upon the religious apprehension of God and his ethical will is further evidenced by Jesus' thought concerning life in the kingdom. The kingdom is to be the kingdom *of God.* Its importance lies not in the fact that omnipotent power is to be placed "at the service of the hatreds and ambitions of the Jewish people,"[37] nor simply in the experience of eternal blessedness on the part of men, nor merely in the vindication of man's prejudices, prides and claims to reward, but in the perfect fulfilment of God's justice and love. It is not a secular goal for social reform but a religious gift of a new society, a gift that would bring to light the inner meaning and purpose of his-

---

37. M. Goguel, *Life of Jesus* (New York, 1933), p. 569.

tory, a level of life in true community that would fulfil man's deepest needs and God's holiness. The kingdom, to use Macmurray's phrase, unites the concrete and the universal.[38] It is neither a this-worldly Utopia to be attained by political-economic-social reforms nor is it an other-worldly transcendentalism.

Jesus anticipated a new and revolutionary this-worldly order. . . . Jesus felt himself the prophet and instrument of the coming of this new order and conducted himself with a fully realistic understanding of the circumstances involved. . . .

The transcendental eschatological element is the counterpart and overtone of the historical element. Jesus' errand was one of this-worldly redemption. The apocalyptic he uses lends a significance, motive and grounding to that redemption that could not otherwise be suggested. . . .

. . . a depth of perspective which includes the ultimate spiritual goal of mankind, but in the foreground . . . a characteristically prophetic concern for this world's future.[39]

D. The Kingdom as Present Reality.

Thus far, Jesus' thought concerning rewards has been set in the framework of his expectation of the Judgment and the kingdom as future events, with the fulfilment of the divine justice postponed until the present interim has passed. The present trend in research is to place stress upon Jesus' faith that the kingdom was even during his ministry "breaking-in" upon human history, that it was even then partially realized. Scholars differ in their interpretation of the precise points and forms in which Jesus experienced the kingdom as being apprehended in the present. The mythological character of all apocalyptic makes difficult the arbitrary separation of present from future aspects, for apocalyptic pictures divine activity as taking place upon a double stage, with events on the earthly plane preceded and determined by events on the heavenly plane. Events which are present and past in the transcendental conflict of God and Satan are still future in their realization within human history.[40] Transcendentally, the kingdom may be considered as present to the extent that God has taken decisive steps in the banishment of Satan and the inauguration of the kingdom, while the historical counterpart of this activity still awaits consummation. Jesus seems to have claimed direct knowledge of these prior steps, present intimations that the ultimate issues had already been determined in God's moral purpose. He saw Satan "falling as lightning from heaven," things which prophets and kings had long hoped to see. In his own expulsion of demons, he sensed the "finger of God," a sign of the kingdom's

---

38. John Macmurray, *Creative Society* (New York, n.d.), pp. 58 f.
39. A. N. Wilder, *op. cit.*, pp. 45, 47, 51. An excellent treatment of the ethic of Jesus as an "eschatological stimulus" revealing the pure will of God is M. Dibelius, *Sermon on the Mount* (New York, 1940), chaps. iv, v.
40. R. Otto, *op. cit.*, chaps. xi–xix; A. N. Wilder, *op. cit.*, Part II.

coming. The prophetic announcement of the kingdom and the call to repentance were organically related to this conviction of the arriving kingdom.[41] In a new way, God's forgiveness and grace were even now operating to make possible a new-covenant relationship with the elect community. As personal representative of the days of the "Son of Man," Jesus was conscious of mediating the divine wisdom, the mystery of the kingdom. He enlisted disciples under the yoke of the new age, and gave them power and authority to carry on their mission of preaching and healing.[42] In the formation of the community of the new covenant and in the ensuing sacrifices of this community he detected an advance stage of historical development, a point of transition from the present age to the future, which was a necessary part of the divine program. The ethical norms by which this community shaped its life were made both necessary and possible by the fact that powers of the end-time were even then being apprehended within the historical process.

The question must therefore he raised: Did this conviction of the partial realization of the kingdom noticeably affect the pattern of expected rewards? Undoubtedly it influenced Jesus' religious experience, his sense of mission, his attitude toward his disciples, his conception of human duty, his criticism of contemporary institutions and his awareness of the need for suffering in this final conflict between the two kingdoms. But his promises of rewards and punishments remain consistently oriented toward the future judgment and the coming age. Man's repentance and renewed obedience were made realizable only because of what God had already done, and they were now motivated by gratitude for his grace which was already available. The new order is already the cause of joy to the poor, the humble meek, the captive, the demon-possessed, those who are persecuted for righteousness' sake. The fulfilment of their hopes is assured, but it is not yet accomplished. The disciples of the kingdom experience a new fellowship, a new confidence of "daily bread" and the necessities of life, a new source of consolation and comfort. But, as Professor Wilder has pointed out, even these rewards are really eschatological and "the strictly eschatological sanctions do not fade into unreality in the least."[43] Jesus' teachings concerning rewards offer insuperable difficulties to Professor Dodd's attempt to interpret the whole of Jesus' thought as "realized eschatology" and to Professor Bultmann's attempt to transcendentalize the kingdom and to absolutize the demands for obedience.[44] Jesus' faith in the presence of the divine powers of the new age provided an opening wedge which the early church used to reconcile the apocalyptic hope with its own continuing historical experience, but it was not incompatible with his own anticipation of future events which would fulfil his announcements of doom and dawn.

41. Matthew 12.25–29; Luke 11.21 f.; 10.17–24; 16.16; 7.18–23; Mark 4.11; Cf. A. N. Wilder, *op. cit.*, pp. 64 f.
42. A. N. Wilder, *op. cit.*, chaps. viii–ix.   43. *Idem*, p. 119.
44. C. H. Dodd, *Parables of the Kingdom* (London, 1935); D. R. Bultmann, *Jesus and the Word* (New York, 1934).

E. Objections to this Interpretation.

The suggestion that Jesus stressed concrete retribution in the Judgment and kingdom arouses vigorous protest in many quarters. The first line of attack is to attribute the gospel passages of an apocalyptic character not to Jesus but to the corrupting influence of early Christians. This attack invariably fails in any close analysis of the gospel tradition, for eschatological sanctions appear in a very large proportion of the sayings. To interpret all such passages as secondary would be such a wholesale purge of gospel sources that there could be little confidence left in any particular strand. Evidence for apocalyptic rewards is found in the earliest written sources and in all types of teaching unit, particularly in those which Form Criticism is finding to be most primitive—pronouncement stories, proverbs, parables, and poetic stanzas. These earliest strata reflect a high degree of consistency in the attitude toward future retribution. Nor should it be forgotten that this cycle of ideas was not the peculiar creation of the early Christians, but is rooted deeply in Jewish tradition and in the thought patterns of the contemporary community. It is an integral part of the earliest Christian preaching by those who had heard Jesus. It would be unjustified violence to the norms of literary and historical criticism to expunge apocalyptic sanctions from the record simply because they seem objectionable to modern Christians.

A second line of attack is grudgingly to accept the presence of this idea of reward in Jesus' teaching, but to interpret it as an archaic hangover that does not represent Jesus' own emphasis. Other passages in the gospels are found that seem to be noneschatological in temper and these are made the touchstone of Jesus' real message. For example, did not Jesus demand obedience to God without any thought of reward but simply as required by man's filial relationship to the divine Father? Is not the truest epitome of Jesus' ethic found in the parable of the servant who has come from his day's work in the field and who continues his duties by serving his lord's dinner? "Even so ye also, when ye shall have done all the things that are commanded you, say, we are unprofitable servants; we have done that which it was our duty to do."[45] Other sayings stress the importance of selfless obedience to the will of God: the first commandment, the love of neighbor, the Golden Rule, the demand for inner purity and sincerity.

The absence of sanctions in such teachings, however, does not signify a contradiction of sanctions used elsewhere. Neither does the appeal to reward in other teachings make them thereby less noble. All Jesus' teachings, with or without such an appeal, center in the need for complete obedience to the will of God. The parable just cited does not deny that the servant will receive recompense; it simply protests against making the desire for immediate reward the sole motive for the service of God. The same may be said of the lofty injunctions to inner purity and the protests in Matthew's sermon against pride,

---

45. Luke 17.7-10.

anger and lust. Jesus does not include sincere desire for the kingdom in his category of impure motives; rather, it is constantly encouraged. The very inducement used to support his demand for purity of thought is the assurance of future recompense.[46]

It is frequently maintained that Jesus' picture of a loving God is incompatible with the picture of a punishing God, that his doctrine of God's grace abrogates the doctrine of God's retribution. God's mercy is, to be sure, central in Jesus' message and mission; but nowhere is it admitted to be inconsistent with his justice. To both Jesus and the Jewish prophets the fulfilment of justice was the highest expression of divine love. The kingdom would be the supreme proof of his mercy, the gift revealing the "Father's good pleasure." Man could not merit the kingdom, but he could enter it only by fulfilling certain definite conditions. For those unjustly oppressed, the promise of a nearby day of reckoning was in fact the assurance that God was still a God of love. Jesus, with many Jewish leaders, realized that during the present age "God lets his sun shine upon the evil and the good," being merciful to the sinner by withholding the merited punishment and prolonging the opportunity to repent. But God's patience would finally be exhausted, as it had been exhausted in other periods of history, and drastic punishment alone would avail to reassert the claims of justice. Finally, God's mercy did transcend the idea of mechanical retribution, in which equal merit insures equal recompense. The glories of the messianic age would far exceed the merit of anyone, and would constitute an equal reward for men with unequal deserts, as the parable of the laborers in the vineyard indicates.[47] But while this denies any rigid legalism, it does not deny that God does reward the repentant and obedient with life in the new age. To Jesus, the future fulfilment of men's hope was just as certain as the existence of a righteous God who acts within history to fulfil his purpose and his covenant promises.

Other objections levied against Jesus' teachings on reward usually involve criticisms applied to the Jewish pattern of faith as a whole. Inasmuch as these have been reviewed in the first chapter, they need not be discussed further here. One of them does require mention, however, for it is a problem which faced the early Christians with unusual force, i.e., the failure of the anticipated historical fulfilment of justice. Jesus' message of the kingdom was not borne out by historical events in precisely the fashion he had anticipated. The Judgment Day did not appear. The kingdom tarried. Thus, his gospel of salvation had to face the frustration which through the ages has dogged the Jewish religious hope. And the decisive event which apparently proved this frustration was again, as it had been in earlier ages, the suffering of the righteous. In this case, it was the death of Jesus himself.

46. Matthew 6.1–20, 33; 5.20–48; 13.44–46; Mark 9.47; Luke 14.12–14. Cf. also C. G. Montefiore, *op. cit.*, II, 529; Pigou, "The Ethics of Jesus," *International Journal of Ethics*, XVII (1907), 281.
47. Matthew 20.1–16.

CHAPTER V

The Early Christian Synthesis

A. The Initial Reinterpretation.

JESUS' faith in the "acceptable year of the Lord" lived on among his followers, motivating their activity. The apocalyptic gospel possessed many elements of potency. It was not simply his own individual dream but represented the age-long hopes of Israel and the Near East. It was a goal thoroughly relevant to the conflicts of his day, expressing in definite, realistic terms the urgent life-needs of multitudes. The band of disciples, recruited largely from these masses who eagerly were awaiting the "day-spring from on high," was united by their expectation of deliverance and by their sharing of the vocation of Jesus. To be sure, his message had disappointed some of them when they found it was not based so much upon immediate steps toward social amelioration as upon the deeper religious faith in divine activity. But his closer associates continued to work with him in preparing the nation for the revolution in human affairs. Even this inner circle, however, was dismayed by his untimely death.

While this event brought sorrow and remorse in the cutting of personal ties, it created a greater crisis for their faith. For Jews were traditionally realistic in accepting the fact of personal death. Death was no terror to them, no great religious problem. But this death was different: this was the death of the anointed prophet of the kingdom, in whose work were focused the authority and powers of the kingdom. His death at a moment of great expectancy undercut the faith by which they lived. Gradually, we know not how soon, their emotions must have coalesced about two inescapable poles of experience, an antithesis which required resolution. One pole centered in their faith, hope and love: faith in God, his moral, communal, historical activity; hope in his kingdom and the fulfilment of his covenant promises; love for Jesus, confidence in his integrity, authority and obedience, and loyalty to their common mission. But the other pole of reality was no less inescapable: the death of Jesus, the triumph of the powers of evil, the delay of the kingdom. The logic of that event cut athwart all that they had hitherto believed.

Clearly there were two alternatives. Either they could surrender their faith-hope-love; or, accepting the death of Jesus, they could maintain those certainties and seek to understand on a deeper level the cruel suffering of their righteous leader. They could renounce their aspirations or, resigning themselves to the tragedy, reinterpret those aspirations in the light of the tragedy. Like Job and the Psalmists they experienced the heightened tension between divine purpose and historical injustice, divine goodness and human sin, divine love and human suffering. It was a problem centuries old, a problem central to Jewish history, a problem which had given rise to the most profound insights of Jewish religion. Facing the ancestral problem in this new form they had the deeply engrained Jewish habit of reinterpreting all historical events religiously. "The bent spring returned." Out of their despair arose a new confidence in God and his kingdom. The prophet Jesus had lost his life, but even that must somehow be integrally related to the divine program of ultimate deliverance.

This reassurance must have been inseparable from the experiences which expressed and corroborated it, i.e., the visions of the risen Jesus. These visions gave them new certainty of the purpose of God, the nearness of the new age and the authority of Jesus. More than that, they disclosed the fact that their prophetic leader had now become Messiah-elect, soon to return to establish the very kingdom which he had proclaimed. With new enthusiasm they announced their message of salvation, "Repent, for the kingdom is at hand." The gospel which Jesus preached was thus made the starting-point for the movement which eventuated after his death. The idea of imminent retribution was the same; Jesus' resurrection only made salvation more certain, more immediate, and more clearly defined. Another stage in the kingdom's ingress had been marked, though by the death of the Messiah. Jesus' death through the hostility of Satan acting through the Romans and priestly leaders had been a Pyrrhic victory for Satan. To the disciples the mystery was revealed: Jesus' death had been a necessary prelude to his Messiahship. Soon he would return for the consummation. Thus Christianity began as a messianic sect among the Jews of Palestine.

B. The Pauline Synthesis.

Within a generation, this new movement was firmly transplanted in the Hellenistic milieu of the far-flung Roman empire, and the necessary reinterpretations brought radical changes in the Christian patterns of expectation. For apocalypticism was not congenial to the new soil. In earlier centuries, to be sure, apocalyptic ideas had circulated widely among the peoples of the Mediterranean, though without the distinctively prophetic orientation that they received among the Jews. But by the first century, these ideas had become quite unintelligible to Hellenists, as evidenced by their neglect among Hellenistic Jews.[1] The process of Christian expansion therefore made necessary basic modifications in the eschatological sanction. The most significant synthesis is found in the religious thought of Paul.

1. Apocalypticism Modified.

The ultimate sanction in Paul's faith is the recompense which will be given men in the day of judgment. He feels himself to be living in the twilight of one era looking forward to the dawn of the next. Upon him and his con-

[1]. W. L. Knox, *St. Paul and the Church of the Gentiles*, chap. i.

temporaries the ends of the ages meet. Before many years Jesus will return, he will "descend from heaven with a shout, with the voice of the archangel, and with the trumpet of God." Then will appear the judgment as a day of fire, in which Christ will administer great rewards and drastic penalties. "Like a thief in the night," sudden destruction will come, "as travail upon a woman with child, and they shall in nowise escape." Enemies of Christ will inherit eternal perdition; those who suffer for him will be given "an eternal weight of glory." Leaders of the church, such as Paul and Apollos, will each receive reward appropriate to his stewardship. The work of individual church members will likewise be tested "as by fire."[2] This confidence in the final judgment as the ultimate touchstone of salvation is in part a survival due to the tradition which Paul inherited, but it is more than a survival; Paul himself yearned incessantly for the coming consummation when corruption would give way to incorruption, longing "for the adoption, the redemption of our body. For we are saved in hope."[3]

To a limited extent, the apostle believes in present material retribution. Civil officers are ministers of God, avengers "for wrath to him that doeth evil." The turmoil and strife of the Gentile world are marks of divine anger. Occasionally he attributes the death of Christians to ritual offences. But this appeal to present recompense is incidental rather than central. Poverty and sickness are no certain signs of God's displeasure, nor is freedom from suffering to be expected in this age.[4]

The function of apocalypticism in Paul's faith differs from that which it served in prophetic Judaism, and the change was due chiefly to the different setting with its different formulation of religious needs. Paul did not face the crucial political, economic, social and religious maladjustments which had molded the thought of John the Baptist and Jesus. He was generally favorable to the Romans and felt the advantages rather than the burdens of their rule. He was not deeply sensitive to the lack of social justice for righteous Jews, nor was he aware of serious clash between wealthy aristocrats and poor pietists. To him the kingdom was significant not as the fulfilment of divine justice but as part of God's foreordained plan for the world. Paul inherited the apocalyptic outlook; it was not a functional, organic emergent from his own situation.

To be sure, as a pre-Christian Pharisee Paul had shared the messianic hope. But his Gentile pessimism concerning the sinfulness of human nature and his Pharisaic zeal for a surpassing righteousness as the requirement of the kingdom had probably served but to deepen his sense of frustration and futility. His

---

2. Romans 1.18; 2.1–16; 3.5 f.; 5.9 f.; 11.22–24; 12.19; 13.5, 11, 12; 14.10; I Cor. 1.18; 3.13, 17; 3.8; 4.5; II Cor. 4.17 f.; 5.10 f.; 6.3 f.; I Thess. 4.5 f.; 5.2 f.; 5.23 f.; II Thess. 1.8–10; Col. 3.5; Phil. 1.28; 3.20 f.; 4.5; cf. F. V. Filson, *St. Paul's Doctrine of Recompense* (Leipzig, 1931); K. Lake, *Earlier Epistles of Paul* (2d ed., London, 1914), p. 437; A. H. McNeile, *St. Paul* (Cambridge, 1920), pp. 268–274.

3. J. Weiss, *op. cit.*, chap. xviii.

4. Romans 1.16 f.; 13.3–6; I Cor. 11.30; cf. F. V. Filson, *op. cit.*

expectations of the new age had probably produced an inner dread rather than buoyant enthusiasm, such as he found in the Christian message of God's grace in inaugurating the kingdom process without respect to human merit. The struggles most real to the conscience of Paul were not so much historical, objective, social, as they were cosmic, subjective, individual. Man's fate as an individual was considered dependent upon the conflict between God and the celestial forces which had enslaved this age, and consequently dependent upon the conflict between man's spirit and his "body of sin and death." It is wholly natural, then, that for him life in the kingdom would represent deliverance from different evils than it had for Jesus.

Positively, the expectation of reward in the new age was modified in four major directions: (1) Eschatology was subtly assimilated with cosmogony, emphasis shifting from events on the historical level to events on the cosmic level, or in the words of Wilfred Knox, "from Omega to Alpha."[5] (2) The future hope was interpreted not as a fulfilment of national, class or group interests but as the fulfilment of individual needs. (3) Correlated with these changes and emerging from the conviction that life in this age is corrupted by its material basis, the kingdom loses many of its secular qualities and becomes transcendentalized and spiritualized. (4) As the kingdom rises above the categories of time, it becomes more nearly possible to conceive it as a present reality, apprehensible now to the men who come within the sphere of its spiritual influences.

The origin and significance of these changes will appear in our discussion of regeneration. But some of them may be illustrated now by reference to Paul's conception of immortality, which clearly represents the fusion of Hebraic and Hellenistic constituents. The factions in the Corinthian church had differed in their beliefs, those with Jewish background contending for a physical resurrection and those with Greek background insisting that immortality would be valueless unless it brought release to the spirit from its carnal prison. With the latter Paul agrees that "flesh and blood cannot inherit the kingdom," but with the former he insists upon the fact of resurrection, not, to be sure, through reanimation of the present physical body, but by miraculous transformation into a spiritual or heavenly body. This new body will be given to all believers, whether dead or alive, at the Parousia.[6]

Such a transformation must await the future triumph of Christ over the enemy spirits now ruling the cosmos. The apostate world-powers must first be reconciled and brought under subjection to God.[7] The last enemy to be subdued will be death, for Paul "the king of terrors, of which he cannot think without a shudder." Man's mortality, the corollary of the reign of evil celestial forces, is the radical evil from which Paul seeks deliverance;[8] to define

---

5. W. L. Knox, *op. cit.*, chap. iv.
6. I Cor. 15.51 f.; cf. also K. Lake, *op. cit.*, pp. 215–219; J. Weiss, *op. cit.*, pp. 531–537.
7. I Cor. 15.24–28; Gal. 4.3, 8–10; 5.1; Col. 1.13; 2.10–15, 20.
8. Romans 8.18–39; W. Morgan, *Religion and Theology of Paul* (Edinburgh, 1917), p. 92; H. R. Willoughby, *op. cit.*, pp. 289–297.

the eschatological hope in these terms individualizes it in a thoroughly Hellenic fashion. Death is conceived in a double sense: final extinction of the individual, and the corruption of man's soul by his sinful body. Consequently, the future hope is not only individualized; it is spiritualized to embody that true, genuine, divine, eternal life whose real antithesis is spiritual rather than physical death.[9] Heaven tends to be pictured in the eternal and ideal character common to Greek philosophy. Finally, all these alterations in the conception of immortality are integrated with the tendency to interpret it as present already in the life of the Christian. Believers are now a new creation, with power over the flesh, unique spiritual endowments, and immediate fellowship with Christ. These present values represent rewards in terms of mystical regeneration, the major Pauline modification in the early Christian view of salvation.

2. Mystical Regeneration Modified.

The major elements in Paul's view of regeneration may be outlined as follows:

Without the gospel man is:	*With the gospel man is:*
A creature of clay living only on a physical plane;	A reborn personality living on a spiritual plane;
an inheritor of the legacy of the first Adam;	an inheritor of the legacy of the second Adam, Christ;
bound by his carnal nature to a life of sin and frustration;	released from carnal chains to a life of righteousness and fulfilment;
helpless under the power of Satan and celestial powers;	given God's power to conquer all the rulers of this age;
alienated from God without the ability to bridge the chasm;	reconciled to God through adoption as his son;
limited to foolish human wisdom which knows not God;	given access to divine wisdom through special revelation;
enslaved to the Law: to the Torah, if a Jew; to the law of nature, if a Gentile;	freed from life under the law to life in the spirit;
tormented by his conscience, suffering mental turmoil;	given the peace of God and a tranquil conscience;
isolated from any enduring community;	elected as a citizen of the true and new Israel, the covenant community;
condemned to frightful punishments, here and hereafter;	assured of joy and bliss, continuing through the judgment;
doomed to death, finally and irretrievably.	translated from death to life, certain and eternal.[10]

9. I Cor. 13.12; 15.47-49; II Cor. 3.18; 4.18; 5.1-4; Phil. 3.20; E. J. Price, "Paul and Plato," *Hibbert Journal*, XVI (1918), 269.
10. Romans 6-8; I Cor. 1.30 f.; II Cor. 4.7-16; 10.3-6; Gal. 5.24 f.; Col. 1.14 f.; 2.11-15.

The redemption experience engenders great emotional exhilaration. In ecstasy the believer is lifted to "the third heaven" in which he has visions of divine things, a special *gnosis* which confers upon him such gifts as prophecy, speaking with tongues, and the working of miracles.[11] These are signs that the rebirth has been effected. But to those who have been reborn, a differentiation of reward is expected. Some may forfeit the gains of their new status, some may remain "babes" in Christ, some may develop into "full-grown men." The original experience is a gift that requires consistent moral endeavor if perfection is to be gained.

Inseparable from the new birth of the Christian is the experience of mystical communion with Christ. He suffers, dies, and rises with Christ. The Holy Spirit, variously described as the Spirit of God and the Spirit of Christ, makes his home in the heart of the believer. Christ lives in him, and he in Christ. Those who share the Spirit of Christ are members of the body of Christ, the new Israel.[12]

These conceptions of salvation as mystical regeneration are closely interrelated and interdependent; they are comprehensive and many-sided—including cosmic, historical, psychological, social, moral ramifications—but they are at the same time remarkably integrated attempts to describe a single continuing experience.

The interpretation of the rewards of the Christian life in terms of regeneration constitutes Paul's greatest modification of the earlier Christian pattern of expectation. This raises the question of the origin of this interpretation. It is clear that Paul did not inherit it from either Palestinian Judaism or primitive Christianity. And while there are some parallels between Pauline sanctions and those of Stoic teachers, the description of mystical regeneration as a whole is foreign to the Stoic gospel. On the other hand, it is significant that every important phase of redemption as offered by the mystery religions has its counterpart in Paul's view of salvation. Both seek deliverance from the same evils; both offer the same satisfactions. The works of Reitzenstein, Cumont, Wendland, Dieterich, W. L. Knox, and Willoughby provide mountains of evidence.

How is this parallelism to be explained? Did Paul consciously copy the rewards of the competing religions in order to outbid them for men's allegiance? Did he incorporate the assurance of regeneration in his message simply to strengthen its appeal to Gentile prospects? It is possible that occasionally as a wise missionary statesman he did this, but it is wholly improbable that his basic message originated in this way. The inner relationship of Paulinism and the Mysteries rests not in the conscious "lifting" of the goal of salvation of the latter but in the common experience of human needs, the common quest for values that were framed in similar thought-forms. Paul's desire for regeneration springs from the innermost core of his being. The sanctions he offers

---

11. I Cor. 1.5 f.; 2.6–16; 8.3 f.; 12–14; Col. 1.9; 1.26 f.; 2.2 f.; Phil. 3.8 f.
12. I Cor. 2.16; Gal. 2.20; Romans 6.1–10; Col. 2.12; J. Weiss, *op. cit.*, pp. 511–526.

others are the ends which he has himself sought. His conversion experience was a typically Hellenistic experience, indicating that his basic religious motives had developed prior to his vision of the risen Lord.[13] The influences of the Hellenistic tradition had already been effective in forming his pre-conversion attitudes—e.g., his cosmology and psychology. Nowhere is this more apparent than in Romans 6–8, in which his own struggles for redemption from the sinful flesh are inseparably merged with his appeal to others to accept his gospel. The apostle is witnessing to his own experience when he writes: "Wretched man that I am! Who shall deliver me from the body of this death?" Take each of the aspects of mystic regeneration outlined above and read the passages which illustrate them; the conclusion is inevitable that each is an expression of his own deepest needs, for which he had found satisfaction in the Christian life. His pronouncements to Gentile audiences were determined not so much by the desire to lure them to conversion by adopting special "bait," as by the compulsion to testify to the values which he had realized in the divine revelation. The emphasis in his letters may have varied in accordance with the hopes of the communities to which they were sent, but his basic attitudes toward the goal of salvation remained the same.

We have outlined the major changes which Paul the Hellenist made in his interpretation of the apocalyptic hope of earlier Jewish Christianity. There now remains the investigation of the adjustments which Paul the Jewish-Christian made in the mystical hope of Gentile Christianity.

(1) Regeneration that centers in communion with Christ is definitely subordinated to the salvation that man receives from the hands of God. Jesus is both son and creature of God, the first-born among many brethren, and his last and necessary act is the transfer of the kingdom to his Father so that God may be "all in all."

The final aim of redemption does not rest in fellowship with Christ, but justification before God, reconciliation with him, peace with God, sharing in the Kingdom of God, participation in the eternity and splendor of the presence of God, of course in company with Christ though the most important thing is, surely, that hidden life with God, the being assimilated to God.[14]

This constitutes an important qualification of the Greek pattern of thought, in that the experience of rebirth is never to be sought in and for its own sake, independent of the will of a transcendent God.

(2) The experience of individual subjective rebirth is also qualified by an objective temporal reference to future historical events. However desirable present mystical experience may be, it is only the "first-fruit." Christians are

---

13. B. W. Bacon, *Christianity Old and New* (New Haven, 1914), pp. 95 f.; F. V. Filson, *op. cit.*, chap. i; S. J. Case, *Evolution of Early Christianity*, p. 354; P. Wendland, *American Journal of Theology*, XVII (1913), 345 f.

14. J. Weiss, *op. cit.*, p. 473.

saved "in hope." Promise, sonship, adoption, inheritance, justification, life, glory—all these terms take their meaning from their relationship to the coming historical consummation. All are in vain if the promise of the kingdom be not fulfilled.[15] The hope of regeneration assumes its meaning for Paul within the framework of the hope for historical fulfilment. This implies that Paul's dualistic pessimism concerning the destiny of society, the world of matter, and the body of flesh is never absolute. They are evil, to be sure, but this had not been true in the beginning nor will it be true in the end.

(3) Again, the present experience of redemption was constantly influenced by the objective temporal reference to former historical events. Rebirth was possible only because of what God had done in the life, death and resurrection of Jesus, the tradition of which Paul had received from his predecessors. Paul knew the quality of the character of Jesus and the nature of his mission. He knew that he had suffered unjustly as an expression of his own and God's love for sinners. Communion with the risen Lord meant participation in actual suffering to extend his revealed purpose. As Professor Weiss exclaims: "Let anyone try to produce a myth (of the mysteries) in which there is present this feature of self-denying devotion, this serving love of sacrifice!"[16] This is but one of many ways in which the Christian tradition filled with new meaning the thought-forms of Hellenism.

(4) The mystic ecstasy of the individual was qualified by the objective reference to the immediate corporate reality of the church. To be "in Christ" was to be a member organically related to the body of Christ. The touchstone of "gifts of the spirit" was their effect upon the health of the whole community. Individual interests were thus subordinated to group interests. A sin against a brother Christian was a sin against Christ. One could not himself achieve the goal of salvation apart from the life of the New Israel.[17]

(5) The goal of rebirth was union with Christ, who was not an unknown and unknowable "X," but a very real, personal, historical Jesus, whose character permeated the true Christian communion. The experience of communion was not so much an interpenetration of personalities as the believer's complete dependence upon Christ and his devotion to him. As Jesus was known for his obedience, this quality must be shared by his follower; as Jesus was a supreme expression of divine love, so the Christian mystic must feel the constraining power of the love of Christ. Consequently, the highest of the gifts of those "in Christ" is the gift of love.[18]

(6) This leads us to the sixth important modification in the Hellenistic pattern of salvation: regeneration is for Paul preëminently a moral experience. There are so many evidences of this in Paul's letters that proof seems unnecessary. Paul's own struggle with sin before and after his conversion experience, his insistence that righteousness is an intrinsic quality of rebirth, his

---

15. *Idem*, pp. 526–531.
16. *Idem*, p. 450.
17. I Cor. 12–14; 8.1–13; Romans 14.
18. I Cor. 13; Weiss, *op. cit.*, pp. 452–455.

subordination of the gift of *gnosis* to the gift of love, his threat that Christians can lose their salvation by acts of pride and lust, his stress upon ethical activity rather than contemplative "revelling in mystical moods," his identification of mystical experience and active vocation as servants of Christ, his final reference of salvation to the tribunal of a just God—all these and others represent distinctive superiorities over the ideas of mystical rebirth in the mysteries.

3. The Process of Fusion.

Paul's view of reward, then, is neither purely Jewish nor purely Hellenistic but an amalgam of the two. The apocalyptic sanction is inherited from his Jewish and Christian background and is conditioned by the Hellenistic religious atmosphere. The appeal to mystical rebirth emerges from his Hellenistic milieu and is conditioned by the Jewish-Christian tradition. The process of modification in each case is an integral part of Paul's own religious experience rather than a result of calculated borrowing. Is there a possibility, then, that Paul achieved within the framework of Christian thought an enduring synthesis of these two patterns of salvation? How may one measure the degree of synthesis? Let us proceed by asking the following questions:

Are gross inconsistencies removed? Is the fusion complete? Are the two strands merely superimposed or inseparably interwoven and interdependent? Are the distinctive values of each preserved? Are the distinctive weaknesses of each avoided? Is the result a genuinely new creation, greater than the sum of its parts? The answers to these questions will be facilitated if we compare in each case the success of Paul with the success of those Hellenistic Jews who sought a similar synthesis.

Minor inconsistencies may and have been detected in Paul's thought, partly because Paul was not primarily concerned with the formulation of a perfectly logical and rational philosophical system and partly because of his penchant for paradoxical and antithetical modes of thought. For example, in his struggle with Judaizers he rejects completely dependence upon the Law and its works, insisting that salvation can only be received through the grace of God apprehended by faith; but in his attack upon antinomianism he returns to the Jewish doctrine of retribution: "Whatsoever a man sows, that shall he also reap." Undoubtedly the apocalyptic and mystical goals of religion are incompatible if each is conceived in its extreme unqualified form, but Paul has so modified both that they become complementary parts of a single process of experience. That such a modification is possible is due to Paul's philosophy of history, in which the kingdom is seen to have both present and future aspects, both integral to a single divine process. The mystical experience of the presence of the kingdom is everywhere oriented toward the future apocalyptic fulfilment. On the other hand, the anticipation of justification at the final judgment is everywhere influenced by the past historical events and by the present activity of the Spirit in the lives of Christians. Proceeding upon the assumption that the mystical and apocalyptic patterns are mutually exclusive, that one is weak to the extent that the other is strong, Professors Weinel and Porter[19] argue that Paul based his religion almost entirely upon the experience of present sonship, while Professors Schweitzer and Johannes Weiss[20] insist that the prevalence of the eschatological hope leaves "very little room for mysticism in his religion." The supposed antithesis upon which these conclusions rest does exist for other Hellenists of Paul's day, but it does not exist for Paul, for he has modified both goals so that they become mutually inclusive rather than exclusive.

This leads to the answer of the second question, the completeness of the fusion. Neither are the sanctions artificially superimposed, as in the writings of Stoic Jews, nor do the Hellenistic sanctions monopolize attention as in the writings of mystic Judaism. Rather, the two are so closely interwoven in the same paragraphs that one can be disentangled only by destroying the unity of the paragraph.[21] The chapters which do not contain both strands in supplementary relationship are few. The interdependence is witnessed by the fact that Paul insisted that Christian redemption is vain either if the past historical activity of Christ is false, or if the present experience of spiritual rebirth is a mirage, or if the future Parousia is fictitious. This interdependence of two strands of thought is in striking contrast with the syncretistic efforts of Diaspora Judaism.

In the process of fusion did Paul appropriate the distinctive values and avoid the distinctive weaknesses of each pattern of expectation? Convincing demonstration at this point is impossible, because each interpreter will have his own conception of the values and weaknesses of the apocalyptic and mystical traditions, dependent in the main upon his own conception of reward and his own philosophy of history. For our purpose, it will suffice to set forth the author's own analysis of the strength and weakness of each separate tradition and then state his own conclusions concerning the effectiveness of the Pauline synthesis.

Distinctive merits of apocalyptic conceptions of reward:

(*a*) The centrality and ultimacy of the historical activity of a transcendent God of justice and mercy.

(*b*) The subordination of realistic pessimism concerning the present age to moral optimism concerning the final triumph of God's purpose. Hope lies "beyond tragedy."

(*c*) The maintenance of the principle of retribution as effective within history, defined not in terms of the mechanical operation of self-existent laws but in terms of the sovereignty of a just but forgiving God.

---

19. H. Weinel, *St. Paul, The Man and His Work* (New York, 1906), p. 342; F. C. Porter, "The Thought of Paul," *Journal of Biblical Literature*, XLI (1922), 198.
20. J. Weiss, *op. cit.*, p. 526.
21. Romans 6.1–14; 8.1–17; II Cor. 6.14–7.1; Gal. 5.24–6.10; Phil. 2.14 f.; Col. 3.1–10.

(*d*) The apprehension of personality as an historical unity, inseparably and organically related to the corporate whole.

(*e*) The interpretation of life in the kingdom as the fulfilment of man's *moral* quest, and therefore as requiring the destruction of the existing order in which that quest is denied fruition.

(*f*) The continuing use of the sanction to support the demand for moral-religious repentance and renewed obedience to a transcendent reality.

The Pauline synthesis preserves each of these as intrinsic qualities of the Christian hope.

Distinctive faults of apocalyptic conceptions of reward:

(*a*) The postponement of all reward to a future age is satisfactory only if that age be considered near-at-hand and not some "far-off divine event toward which the whole creation moves." The denial of all satisfactions in the present age may serve only to deepen the frustrations which the apocalyptic hope seeks to alleviate.

(*b*) The probability that the apocalyptic expectation, when removed from the original situation in which it is wholly indigenous, becomes a field for fantastic speculation unrelated to the real issues of life, confusing rather than clarifying the later situation. By its very nature, the apocalyptic frame of reference is less easily transferred to alien cultures than are the legalistic and mystical patterns.

(*c*) The materialistic and prudential definition of the life in the kingdom, fully ethicized when intrinsically related to the moral order and ultimately subordinated to the fulfilment of God's will, is easily perverted into an external appeal to "arbitrary lures and menaces."[22]

(*d*) The apparent failure of the eschatological promise to be fulfilled in the succeeding nineteen centuries, its oversimplification of the achievement at the end of history.

It would be unwise to claim that Paul permanently eliminated these defects of apocalypticism, but they are undoubtedly mitigated by his interpretation. The emphasis upon the past and present redemptive activity of God in Christ, the moral basis and content of the kingdom hope, the spiritualized nature of life in the kingdom, and the voluntary acceptance of suffering not merely as the basis for claim to future compensation but as participation in the divine plan of redemption through Christ, these all prevent the apocalyptic hope from degenerating into idle speculation, immoral compensation, artificial projection of desires, and an exploded dream. At these points and others, the experience of rebirth into the present life of the kingdom of Christ serves to strengthen the future hope in the kingdom of God.

22. A. N. Wilder, *op. cit.*, p. 160.

Distinctive merits of mystical regeneration:

(*a*) The penetrating analysis of human personality, with full awareness of the depths of human sin and of its perennial corrupting of the very springs of human conduct. The sense of sin is so strong that its basis is traced to the very nature of man, to his creation, to his implication in the whole process of nature, and to the domination of demonic forces.

(*b*) The insistence that the fulfilment of life involves the quest for the highest light and truth, bringing satisfaction to the mind as well as the heart, that salvation must include conferring of knowledge concerning the nature of the world and man.

(*c*) The awareness of the profound importance of some direct rapport between the individual and God as the basis of certainty and hope. If God's grace is real, it must make a difference here and now in the struggle of men to find life's meaning.

(*d*) The frank use of mythology to symbolize and dramatize those aspects of experience less conducive to precise, literal, and logical definition.

Little proof is needed that each of these distinctive values of the mysteries as contrasted from Judaism is incorporated in Paul's religion.

It is even more significant that the distinctive weaknesses of mysticism are corrected at least in part by the apostle. Four of these weaknesses have already been outlined (cf. above, pp. 26–28), each of which receives marked modification. Paul is an individualist, seeking the goal of immortality, but that goal is everywhere made dependent upon the fulfilment of the social, cosmic and historical process. Life in Christ is life in Christ's community. In comparison with the normal Jewish pattern of reward, Paul is a subjectivist, but his subjectivism is qualified by references to objective events in the past, present, and future, and to the objective reality of the church. He is a dualist in the area of psychological, epistemological, and metaphysical analysis, but his dualism is ultimately transcended by a monistic theology and an assurance that a single purpose runs through history from beginning to end. He does not in any sense share the typically Hellenistic conviction of the meaninglessness of human history, nor the extreme relativism of human ethical behavior, nor the scepticism concerning the worth of concrete human institutions and movements. In Hellenistic mysticism and gnosticism, the optimistic assurance of immediate communion with deity could never quite eradicate the feeling of the ultimate futility of the historical process. In Pauline apocalyptic, Hellenistic pessimism concerning the present age is transcended by the confidence in the reality, power, and grace of God, operating to redeem the whole of life, cosmic, historical, communal, moral. Hellenistic Jewish writers did not thus avoid the defects of the mystical quest for salvation.

Paul's theology thus represents a genuine synthesis, greater than the sum of its parts, a synthesis based upon sound insights, and fully incarnated in the whole religious struggle of the man himself. The greatness of this synthesis is manifested by two observations from later Christian history. (1) It was so difficult a synthesis of such basic and divergent patterns, that few of Paul's contemporaries and immediate successors achieved the same degree of interrelatedness. (2) It was so successful in mingling the best elements in Jewish and Hellenistic cultures that in the crucial periods of church history, when similar syntheses have been demanded, Pauline thought has constituted a source of power and truth. The first of these observations receives discussion here. The second rests on evidence that reaches beyond the scope of this study.

C. Early Failures to Maintain the Synthesis.

1. Apocalypticism Unmodified.

One major tendency in the post-Pauline church consisted in the accentuation of the eschatological sanction. When the church faced a crisis in the area of social, economic and political interests, the future hope flourished, while the prevalence of harmonious relations between church and state, and the development of power, prestige, and wealth of the church tended to discourage millenarian excitement. Generally speaking, early Christian apocalypses were occasioned by the rise of persecution and filled the function of "control-literature."[23] The ultimate and most frequent inducement for enduring persecution was the assurance of abundant reward in the coming age, while apostasy was discouraged by the threat of direst penalties.[24] No Christian who became disloyal could ever be readmitted into the number of the saved,[25] while the worst kind of anguish was reserved for the enemies of Christ who persecuted his saints.

Christian leaders interpreted history to support their arguments. Christian martyrs were members of a long line of heroes who had "fought the good fight of faith." The stories of the trials of the prophets, of Christ, of Paul and the other apostles were constantly retold for the benefit of Christians. All great heroes of the Christian faith had suffered, had maintained their faith unshaken, had testified openly, had received certain witness to their reward, and had accomplished great things for the divine cause. They had not yet entered into their reward, but they had been given indubitable assurances that their reward had been laid up in the new age.[26]

Apocalyptists who were faced with critical problems within the church likewise used the promise of future reward in these situations: the threat of false prophets, the prevalence of heretical doctrines, the ambition of church officers,

---

23. Cf. D. W. Riddle, *The Martyrs* (Chicago, 1931), pp. 25 f.
24. Revelation 2, 3, 6, 14, 20–22; Hebrews 3.1–14; 6.18 f.; 10.35–39; 12.8–10; 13.13 f.; I Peter 1.6–9; 2.20–24; 3.13–21; 4.1–19.
25. Hebrews 6.6 f.; 10.31; 12.25–29; Revelation 7.14–17; 9.5; 13.10; 15.21; 20.4–6, 12–15.
26. James 5.10; Hebrews 11; I Timothy 6.13; I Peter 2.21 f.; 3.18; 4.1 f.; II Peter 3.15; Hebrews 2.9 f.; 4.15; 5.7–9; Mark 8.31–38; 10.28–31. Cf. D. W. Riddle, *op. cit.*, pp. 182–197.

the envy of the laymen, the conflict between wealthy and poor within the church. The expectation of the coming judgment is constantly used among those who served Christ.

The unmodified appeal to the eschatological sanction, however, tended to magnify its defects in ways which both Jesus and Paul had avoided. No longer an indigenous product of the total experience of Christians, it tended to become an inherited frame of reference devitalized and degenerate. Nevertheless, it continued to express genuine faith in the underlying moral order of the universe and the ultimate triumph of justice and peace.

2. Regeneration Unmodified.

The second major tendency in the later New Testament period was the increasing use of the Hellenistic goal of rebirth, less and less qualified by any true synthesis with the insights of apocalypticism. In general, this tendency was most apparent among Christians who were most sensitive to the idealistic, gnostic and mystical interpretations of the human problem and who were relatively prosperous and secure in their economic, social and political relationships. The most extreme development of the use of this sanction in the New Testament period is represented by the gospel of John, which "reveals a religious philosophy as deeply imbued with Greek ideas as Philo's."[27]

In Johannine theology, the promise of eternal life appears as the ultimate sanction.[28] Jesus and the Jewish apocalyptists expected that the future life in the kingdom would be a prolongation of the life of "the quick" and a revivification of the dead, rather than an essential metaphysical change in the individuals who participated. John believes that entrance into eternal life comes solely through a spiritual rebirth. Paul had expected this metamorphosis when Christ arrived to usher in the kingdom. John teaches that the new status is entirely a present reality, attainable immediately. For Paul the present was a foretaste of the future; for John it is a real participation in the life which was, is, and shall be. For Paul, the Judgment Day was a concrete historical event; for John it takes place in the immediate decision of the individual. The believer escapes judgment; the unbeliever is already judged and condemned.[29] The ultimate sanction for Paul was eschatological reward; for his successor it is the present status as son of God, life in the light.

Thorough-going dualism dominates John's thought. Corporeal and incorporeal existence are completely antagonistic to each other. The physical world, which is entirely under the control of Satan, is completely opposed to the world of the Spirit. All men are divided into two groups: "that which is born

27. B. W. Bacon, *Gospel of the Hellenists* (New York, 1933), pp. 353, 337 f.; F. C. Porter, *Journal Biblical Literature*, XLI (1922), 191 f.; E. F. Scott, "The Hellenistic Mysticism of the Fourth Gospel," *American Journal of Theology*, XX (1916), 347 f.; R. Reitzenstein, *Die hellenistischen Mysterienreligionen* (Leipzig, 1910), p. 393.

28. The use of life as a sanction appears more than 45 times. Cf. I John 2.17, 25; 5.11 f., 20; John 3.16, 36; 4.36; 5.24; 8.21–24; 11.25 ff.; 12.24 ff.; 15.1; 20.31, etc.

29. John 1.12 f.; 3.18, 36; 5.24; 6.47; 8.38–44; I John 2.15, 29; 3.3–12.

of the flesh," "that which is born of the spirit." Men who live according to the flesh suffer its universal accompaniments: ignorance, falsehood, darkness, sin, mortality. Twice-born men enjoy the new life of the Spirit and of sonship, abiding in knowledge, truth, light and love. The believer has a constant and perfect union with God. God dwells in him, and he in God. He is enabled to see God, to know him, to understand divine secrets. "This is life eternal, to know thee, the only true God."[30]

For John, the present activities of Christ are stressed to the virtual neglect of his past activity and to the exclusion of his future activities. Jesus constantly bestows on his children blessings: the presence of the Comforter, the power to perform great works, the answer to all prayers, fellowship in the light, sacramental cleansing, constant mystical communion, freedom from "the world, the flesh and the devil," the fellowship of the church,—all these are embraced in the concept of life eternal.

The tendency represented in John is in the direction of complete adaptation of Hellenistic patterns of thought without the correction offered by Jewish faith. The weaknesses which have been noted in the mystery religions, and which Paul to a high degree counteracted, reappear in John but slightly affected by Jewish-Christian apocalypticism. No other early Christian produced so genuine and productive a synthesis of the two sanction systems as did Paul.

Since this study was completed, a parallel analysis of salvation systems during the Hellenistic period has appeared in the monumental work of A. J. Toynbee, *A Study of History*. Much in Professor Toynbee's interpretation corroborates and supplements the position outlined in the preceding pages. In Volume VI, Professor Toynbee reduces Hellenistic gospels of deliverance to four: archaism, futurism, detachment, and withdrawal-and-return. Jewish futurism, as represented by Zealots and apocalyptists, is subjected to penetrating criticism along the lines suggested in Chapter I above. Similarly, Hellenistic gospels of detachment, as represented by Stoicism and in part by the mysteries, are shown to be inadequate on many grounds. Early Christianity presented the most profound type of salvation in its message of a kingdom of God which is in history but not of history, a message of divine help mediated through an experience of withdrawal-and-return. Professor Toynbee rightly concludes that the real transition between the Jewish gospel of futurism and the early Christian message of salvation by withdrawal-and-return was marked by the death and resurrection of Jesus. Personally, Professor Toynbee seems to be nearer to Johannine than to Pauline philosophy of history; nevertheless, his work furnishes extensive documentation for the conclusion that the early Christian gospel possesses unique validity and enduring worth.[31]

30. I John 2.4–3.12; 4.12, 15–21; John 1.12–18; 6.36, 53; 8.38–47; 14.20–23; 15.1–16; 16.13 ff.; etc.
31. A. J. Toynbee, *A Study of History* (New York, 1934–1938), esp. VI, 49–175.

Epilogue

THE conclusion to which the foregoing evidence points is that Paul achieved a more complete synthesis of Jewish and Hellenistic conceptions of the goal of life than did either the Diaspora Jews or other early Christian writers. It is not claimed that his solution of the problem of reward constitutes a perfect and final synthesis, but it was a true and productive synthesis. And that was no small achievement, for Paul was dealing with two antithetical modes of thought: the Jewish faith in historical, social fulfilment and the Hellenistic denial of significance to the social and historical process. It has been noted that the greatest defect in the Jewish pattern was revealed by the recurring failures and successive postponements of expected rewards, culminating for Christians in the death of Jesus. In contrast, the Hellenistic promises were vulnerable because the denial of the possibility and value of historical fulfilment lead to complete subjectivism, ultimate scepticism and futility. Paul's dilemma in defining the Christian goal of salvation lay in the fact that he was confronted with two incompatible philosophies of history, each of which was unsatisfactory, and neither of which could be wholly relinquished. Only a genius could fuse such opposite world-views without superimposing one on the other in illogical fashion or permitting one to dominate the other. Only a genius could preserve so many of the strengths of both while escaping so many of their weaknesses.

Paul's reconciliation of the two was impossible on the purely logical level; it was possible only through the adoption of a mythological and dialectical philosophy of history which is expressed in his view of the kingdom of God. Life in the kingdom is for Paul neither wholly present nor wholly future, but at once both present and future in essential interdependence. The kingdom has drawn near to men, its inception has already been marked by definite historical events, its mysteries have been revealed, and its powers have been released through the work of Christ and his presence in the new community. But these present manifestations are partial and fragmentary, resting upon the certainty of a future, universal and historical consummation of the righteous purpose of God. Man is saved by grace in the present order, but this salvation is organically related to a process which culminates in a final judgment in which every man will receive recompense according to his works.

The factors in Paul's experience that contributed to the forging of this new unity are partially hidden from modern analysis, but they can be partially disentangled. Paul could not have arrived at his dialectical theology if he had not been reared in a Hellenistic Jewish environment. The fusion could not have been so genuine had he not himself sought immediate rebirth from the life of sinful and mortal flesh and at the same time shared eagerly in the Pharisaic quest for justification in the final assize. Nor could the solution have been so indigenous to the Christian tradition had not Jesus announced the presence of the kingdom in his own mission, had not the early disciples experienced the first-fruits of kingdom life in the work of the Spirit, had they not been able to reinterpret the death of Jesus as one of the decisive steps in the program of divine redemption. The synthesis was also due in part to the necessities of leadership of the Pauline communities. Paul was sensitive to the concrete problems which resulted from the Jewish insistence upon legal righteousness as a road to the kingdom; he was equally aware of the logical ethical implications of the Gentile Christian assurance that salvation was complete in present rebirth into the kingdom. Even though full weight be given to the environmental and traditional conditions, there must be added a recognition of the authenticity of Paul's personal religious life and the profundity of his theological insights.

It has been suggested that one criterion of the fruitfulness of Paul's synthesis is the fact that in succeeding generations, when a similar dilemma has confronted Christians, there have been perennial returns to the thought of Paul. To illustrate or to prove that conviction would require volumes; there is need, however, to suggest the existence of a similar dilemma in present thought and the relevance of early Christian teachings to modern attempts at a solution. Today, as in the first century, Christians are proclaiming antithetical gospels of salvation, and these conflicting gospels are inherent in antithetical philosophies of history; these interpretations of the meaning of history are formulated in antithetical conceptions of the kingdom of God. Is the fulfilment of life in the kingdom dependent upon future events in the social process, or is realization possible irrespective of those future events?

The reaffirmation of the Jewish tradition is to be found most clearly expressed by writers who share the Marxist analysis of the contemporary situation and the Marxist goal of a classless society.[1] The kingdom of God is equated with this goal, and all salvation awaits the imminent dawn of the era in which justice, equality and freedom will for the first time be realized. There is a direct historical continuity between this idea of salvation and the faith of Jewish prophets, apocalyptists, and Jesus; in some writers recognition of this continuity is fully expressed.

The eternal purpose, the ultimate goal, always present in the mind of God, slowly operates in and upon the evolving world; it penetrates, and is apprehended by, the mind of man, and thus becomes conscious. It attains full expression in Jesus, who knows of what man is capable and that his destiny is to constitute with his fellows a perfect society. Man is only truly himself in an ideal society. Therefore it is in the Beloved Community that the Ideal is realized, that social evolution reaches its goal.[2]

---

[1]. Cf. John Macmurray, *Creative Society; A Clue to History;* John Lewis, ed., *Christianity and the Social Revolution* (New York, 1936), pp. 74–102, 473–504.

[2]. J. Lewis, *op. cit.*, p. 478; cf. also J. Macmurray, *Clue to History*, pp. 42 f., 100.

Epilogue

All Hellenistic dualisms are emphatically rejected as in irreconcilable opposition to this apprehension of the purpose of God. The Pauline synthesis is neither possible nor valid. "It contains a radical inconsistency which cannot be explained away as complementary aspects. Its world-affirming (Jewish apocalyptic), world-denying (Hellenistic) elements are incompatible."[3] Attempts at synthesis are interpreted as rationalizations of "the fatal dilemma of a class society," providing a necessary opiate during the period before objective conditions have made a classless society possible. But the necessary opiate becomes vicious in the present period in which the new society is being born, and it will become wholly useless when the kingdom of a classless society has been ushered in. To the extent that Christianity now offers to men the Hellenistic promises of subjective, individualistic fulfilment in the present age, to that extent it becomes an anti-revolutionary force, a degenerate spiritualistic escape,[4] analogous to the attempt of Christian Science to escape physical sickness by ignoring its reality, thus preventing the removal of the causes and aggravating the disease from which it seeks release. Only by loyalty to the new order and by sacrificial obedience to its demands may Christianity hope to fulfill the purpose for which God brought it into existence. Only thus will the true reward be realized, when the meek inherit the earth.

"The apocalyptic crisis has descended upon our age, not prematurely as in the time of Jesus, but in the fullness of time. Opportunity as it now confronts us is also the final sifting of chaff from wheat, the day of judgment."[5]

The history of Jewish and early Christian apocalypticism throws into relief the perennial values of this revolutionary gospel. Does that history also illuminate the perennial defects? "No," answer the avowed Marxists. The gospel of a future kingdom, they believe, was premature in the first century; but the changed objective conditions of the twentieth century provide a more certain ground for the message "Repent, for the kingdom of God is at hand." We have noted that it was the intransigence of history in failing to fit apocalyptic blueprints which in earlier days forced reinterpretation of the gospel. It should not be surprising, then, that the recent development of fascism with its unexpected frustration and opposition to the classless society has placed Marxists in the same dilemma; nor is it surprising that the history of the Soviet regime should force many former enthusiasts into a new awareness of the impossibility of a full consummation of the kingdom of God within the social-historical process.

It is noteworthy that the Marxist reinterpretation of their hope in the light of unexpected events follows the pattern of early Christian reinterpretations. Fascism itself, though undesired and unexpected, though it represents the supreme attempt of the old order to resist the new, becomes a revelation of the

---

3. Lewis, *op. cit.*, p. 97; cf. also Macmurray's complete renunciation of dualism, *Clue to History*, chap. 2.
4. Lewis, *op. cit.*, pp. 479–501.   5. *Idem*, p. 102.

inevitability of the communist goal. And the temporary delay of the perfect society in Russia is conceived as a necessary interim, in which the "kingdom" is partly present and partly future, the two in interdependence.

Can the dilemma between future hope and present frustration be satisfactorily resolved in this fashion? Whatever may be the reader's attitude, he will find that the defects of the apocalyptic idea of reward as outlined above (pp. 15 f., 64) have a striking applicability to this present problem. They constitute a challenge which Marxist Christians must face.

An opposite tendency in current thought is found among those who accent the validity of the Hellenistic inheritance of Christianity, and who consequently move in the direction of denying meaning to history. Like the Marxists, they find the truly Christian philosophy of history in the message of the kingdom, but this kingdom is viewed only in its present and transcendental aspects. Salvation becomes oriented wholly in terms of present decision on the basis of the immediate revelation of a wholly transcendent God who himself has provided the means for the fulfilment of man's quest. Representatives of this tendency, of course, vary in the degree to which they affirm this view of the Christian gospel. All of them find it difficult to escape completely from the apocalyptic strain in the Christian tradition, and few of them can be satisfactorily labeled. For our purposes, however, the books of Professor C. H. Dodd will suggest the nature and direction of this tendency.[6]

Professor Dodd takes care to distinguish Christianity from Platonic idealism and from Gnosticism in their denial of meaning to the historical process. He insists that Christianity is an historical religion because it finds in history the primary field of divine revelation, and because certain events—the coming, death and resurrection of Jesus—are unique and final events in which God revealed his kingdom.[7] The message of Jesus centers in "realized eschatology," pointing to an End that is "no longer an event in history. It lies beyond this order of time and space."[8] Jesus himself did not seek a definite social-historical goal for men of his day, but "stood isolated among the movements of His time. He took no side in the conflict of ideals."[9] He simply sought to proclaim an act of God in introducing his kingdom to men, a transcendental present kingdom which involved immediate judgment, apart from change in social order. "The teaching of Jesus is not an ethic for those who expect the speedy end of the world, but for those who have experienced the end of this world and the coming of the Kingdom of God."[10] But this kingdom "is altogether

---

6. C. H. Dodd, *Parables of the Kingdom* (London, 1935), *Apostolic Preaching* (Chicago, 1937), *History and the Gospel* (London, 1938), also essay in H. G. Wood, ed., *The Kingdom of God and History* (London, 1938).
7. C. H. Dodd, *History and the Gospel*, chap. i.
8. C. H. Dodd, *The Kingdom of God and History*, p. 22.
9. C. H. Dodd, *History and the Gospel*, p. 123.
10. *Idem*, p. 125.

other than the relativities of human existence." History is completely real only at the point in which "the eternal reality is completely expressed," and this point now lies in the past rather than the future. "The true eschaton, the event in which its meaning is conclusively revealed, has become an object of experience."[11]

Thus, for Professor Dodd, salvation is historical only because it has been revealed in unrepeatable and final events in the past. The triumph of the human struggle does not await a future judgment day but is implicit in the events which already have revealed the "end" of history. Consequently, "when we pray, 'Thy Kingdom come,' we are not praying that at long last history may end with Utopia or the millennium but that in *this* situation in which we stand the reign of God may be made manifest. . . . The future . . . is not our concern."[12] This approach necessitates a dualistic view of human history, a contrast between secular history, which as Professor Dodd admits is a "ding-dong battle," and sacred history in which the transcendent meaning of the whole process has already been revealed in Christ. This complete fulfilment of sacred history in Jesus constitutes a "shattering modification of the prophetic view of history . . . made necessary by events."[13]

Evaluating this position in terms of its gospel of salvation, it is hard to avoid the conclusion that it is much nearer to the Johannine point of view than to the Pauline, and that it represents a surrender of the genius of the religion of Jesus and Judaism in its denial of the meaning of the redemption of society within history and at the end of history.

"Thy kingdom come." Both Professors Macmurray and Dodd pray for it, but to one it is wholly future and social, to the other it is wholly present and primarily individual. The early Christian parallel would be that provided by Revelation and the Fourth Gospel. Are there modern Christians who accept both horns of this dilemma and strive for a more thoroughgoing synthesis? It is significant that there are and that they follow more or less closely the dialectic pattern of Paul's thought.

Professor Reinhold Niebuhr, in his book, *Beyond Tragedy*, seeks to define and illustrate

Christianity's dialectical conception of the relation of time and eternity, of God and the world, of nature and grace. . . . It affirms the meaning of history and of man's natural existence on the one hand, and on the other insists that the centre, source and fulfilment of history lie beyond history.[14]

For him, the kingdom of God is "not of this world," yet it is at the same time "of this world."[15] The kingdom transcends history, as God himself transcends his creation; but at the same time the kingdom constantly enters into

---

11. C. H. Dodd, *Kingdom of God and History*, p. 26.
12. *Idem*, pp. 37–38.   13. *Idem*, p. 34.
14. Reinhold Niebuhr, *Beyond Tragedy* (New York, 1937), p. ix.
15. *Idem*, pp. 274–278.

history, constituting "a more dangerous peril to the kingdoms of the world than any competing kingdom." It is "relevant to every moment of history as an ideal possibility and as a principle of judgment upon present realities" and it points to ultimate triumph at the end of history.[16] The symbol of this faith is the resurrection hope, which preserves the necessary conviction of the solidarity of body and soul, the organic relationship of the individual to society, and the recognition that "individual life always transcends the social process as well as being fulfilled in it."[17]

Another scholar seeking a similar synthesis is Paul Tillich. The basic elements in his philosophy of history appear in his definition of the kingdom of God, which he uses as a symbolic expression of the ultimate meaning of existence.

The meaning of history can be found neither in a final stage of historical development—the ultimate fulfilment of all historical potentialities—nor in an infinite approximation to a fulfilment which can never be reached, nor in a continuous change of historical growth and decay as found in nature, nor in a transcendent supra-nature unconnected with history. . . .

The ultimate meaning of history is the supra-historical unification and purification of all elements of preliminary meaning which have become embodied in historical activities and institutions. . . .

In this way historical activity acquires ultimate importance without becoming utopian, and the supra-historical acquires content without becoming mythological.[18]

Modern Christian prophets and teachers are confident of the fulfilment of the promise "And great shall be your reward." They are agreed that underlying this promise is the insistent divine demand, "Seek ye first the kingdom of God and His righteousness." They unite in their faith that the vocation of the church is to announce and mediate the life of this kingdom to the world, that the church is called to this mission by the historical Jesus. Their experience within this community points to a fulfilment of life which is now imperfectly realized. Their differences in defining the nature and value of reward indicate the lack of finality of any early Christian formulation, but they also demonstrate the enduring vitality and profundity of early Christian apprehensions of the meaning of human experience, interpreted in the light of the purpose of God, who was "in Christ reconciling the world unto Himself."

16. *Idem*, pp. 284–286. 17. *Idem*, pp. 289–306.
18. Paul Tillich in H. G. Wood, *Kingdom of God and History*, pp. 113–119.

www.ingramcontent.com/pod-product-compliance
Lightning Source LLC
Chambersburg PA
CBHW070059100426
42743CB00012B/2594